AHMED SALEH EBRAHIM

Enrich your life

Like tycoons

READ2LEAD, for Publishing and Distribution: Address: Office 2942 / 29th Floor, United Tower / Building 316, Road 4609, Complex 346 / Bahrain Bay / Manama / Kingdom of Bahrain

First edition

Illustration by Hanan Al Nakheelan
Translation by arapenz.com
Proofreading by Fatima Al- Sahaf and arapenz.com
Typesetting by Hassan Mohamed, arapenz.com

Contents

Preface

One of the most significant things that has occupied my mind in years is the interest of a vast number of people in money and wealth. This is evident in their conversations and their many visits to websites, as well as the number of million views in social networks. Even if they do not explicitly talk about it, money remains their main concern.

Most people have their curiosity roused to action on how to get money, make a fortune, and be rich. Money is an essential way to feel happy, comfortable and stable. Money is lifeblood. What rouses more the curiosity of people is how others earn their lot and become wealthy.

People have worked for money. Some have become too wealthy that they are soaked in luxury and excesses. Some have earned money enough to get by. Some, however, have toiled but have been living with mouth-to-hand existence. Still, others do not know how to earn money.

Some of those who have worked hard for the money and acquired vast fortune have decided to share their success with others. All people need money and they, in particular, know the ways that have led them to wealth.

Those who desire to pursue wealth can learn from those who have made it. This has led us to search for the rich and famous, who are recognized by the Forbes Magazine as the world's billionaires.

This book contains 15 pivotal points about the lives of nine of some of the world's wealthiest. They were well chosen to be characters of inspiration for this book. They have been selected solely for their fields of specializations.

The characters selected to enrich us are **Warren Buffett, Richard**

Branson, Jack Ma, Elon Musk, Mark Cuban, Larry Page, Oprah Winfrey, Howard Schultz, and Jeffrey Bezos. Our in-depth research into their lives include their humble beginnings, their diaries, their education and work, their experience, their central stations, their mindsets, their philosophy, and their secret success.

In this book, you will find everything you need to know about the secrets and origins of wealth, and how to achieve them through the lives of these nine outstanding world figures, who raked in a total fortune of $317.8 billion in 2018.

After relying upon Allah, crystalizing the idea, and choosing the nine remarkable financial influencers of the world, I decided to put together the ideas into a book. My ultimate goal in writing this book is to fulfill my desire to help my colleagues working in my organizations by clarifying the vision on the path to richness.

I have sought the help of my colleagues in the organization and gathered a group of people I trust in doing research for the completion of **"Enrich Your Life Like Tycoons."** The team painstakingly spent almost two years of research, discussed the pros and cons of the book contents, and provided me with pieces of advice on putting this book to bed.

Now, dear reader, prepare yourself for the finest read in the world. The information hidden from you in the past is now out to help you achieve your dream of a life befitting of a tycoon.

Ahmed Saleh Ibrahim

June 30, 2018

1

Rules of Wealth

Introduction:

The most important responsibility of a person who aspires for a prosperous future is to establish a team and an organization of growth, stability and sustainability. This task is required to be carried out in the face of the various challenges, threats, risks, both expected and unexpected. At the same time, one must be ready to seize the opportunities available that can lead to achieving this goal in the time of prosperity, and then proceeding to accomplish the next goal, which grows steadily in all areas. These two goals require significant efforts and great focus.

A person's success in achieving his vision, by reaping the wealth he aspires for, makes him a value to others. Wealth means that a single person, or a representative of an organization, is in a situation that contains abundant quantities of something desirable; for example, knowing how to make money and sustain it. Wealth refers to a valuable thing whether material, or moral. Moral wealth comes from the clarification of the individual and national spiritual values, while material wealth refers to money, real estate such as buildings and lands, and other goods.

A wealth owner achieves prosperity for himself through wealth, which makes him act away from pressure at all times. Wealth refers to money or/and assets. Wealth can come quickly and go quickly.

Many organizations look up to the rich to lead them, as they are the support of the organization; unlike those who have nothing, as they may lack the leadership, the skills and the means to achieve abundance and wealth to the organization. Therefore, it is clear that the quest of the leader to obtain material and moral wealth is very important. The existence of the material wealth of money enables us to achieve moral wealth and give full commitment to its development.

Here, we will review the most important thing the ambitious person needs to achieve his desire of harvesting wealth one day, which is to know the relationship between his financial management and the importance of abundance and freedom to achieve this. Therefore, his decisions have to be neutral, and not to be under the influence of anyone, as well as he who wants this, must have the freedom to act in time to do what he wants, not to only earn his livelihood.

The Basic Concepts and Relationships in The Science of Wealth

The concept of "abundance" is one of the most important pillars to help a person achieve prosperity and progress. It is the concept that is represented in the situation in which something is abundant more than what is usual, which is to the extent of surplus and unlimited gifts. The mindset of "abundance" comes when a person feels secured and valued. This happens when he believes that there is enough for all, which makes his mindset open to all the possibilities and alternatives available to be able to make a wise decision in light of these elements.

On the other hand, there is a paradoxical concept, which is called "scarcity," which is represented in the human beings' possession of unlimited desires in a world of limited resources that does not have sufficient productive capacity to satisfy those desires. The law of "scarcity" explains the inability to pursue more than one goal at the same time. It leads us to trade between these goals and just selects only

one of them. The owners of the mindset of "scarcity" see that there is not enough in this worldly life, as if there is one cake left for everyone, and if one wants to take the biggest piece of it, then there will not be enough of it for others.

Although "scarcity" is something to be dealt with, rather than shunned away from- a person who wants to build his fortune in light of "abundance" will be able to survive and grow, and he who tries to build his fortune in light of "scarcity" will have to declare a state of emergency, and he may ultimately announce his surrender, due to increased risks, threats, and limited resources.

All creatures seek to earn their lot, and God made man with the freedom to uplift his life and manage his own affairs within the Creator's laws. For anyone seeking to enrich himself with money is the right thing. Because money is the lifeblood, it is not surprising that people are preoccupied with it, and it is not strange for them to dispute over it. It is the reason they live, and it is the guarantor of the continuation of the human race, and even a measure where people are classified. It is very natural that they love it, or to reject it.

Wealthy people, who know how to make money and have the ability to do well in financial matters consistently have a comprehensive view of money and toward those who do not have the money. This view is different from those who do not have money; those who do not have money have a different limited view toward money because they do not own it.

Because you aspire, dear reader, to build a fortune, you will inevitably deal a lot with money. It will guarantee you that fortune, in turn, will achieve two goals: survival and growth. Therefore, you have to closely know the relationship between people and money, as well as the view of each toward the other.

3

The Rich and Noble's View of Money

- They love money, love who owns it, love its resources, and learn how to get it.
- They see themselves deserving the money they have, and even think they deserve more.
- They use money to improve their lives and the lives of others around them and promote them.
- They look at money as abundant and enough for all; thus, they are not afraid to give.
- They are open to what fortunes provide for them and are ready to receive all the fortunes offered by life.
- They are always prepared to work, and their actions create prosperity for them.
- They look for sources that bring them money, and they are not those who work for them.
- They are adventurers, who do not fear poverty, and are not afraid of wealth, because money drives and directs their lives.

The Poor and Their View of Money

- They love money and wish for it. They ignore its sources and do not learn how to bring it.
- They believe that money is worth working for; therefore, they work for the money and not for their goals.
- They think that getting money is rare, and what is available of it is not enough for everyone. They are afraid of giving money to others; thus, they will not lose money in case of not giving others what they have.
- They consider saving money to be the priority over improving their lives and the lives of others around them.
- They evade opportunities offered by life to receive fortunes.

- They believe that everyone cannot become rich, and there is not enough money for all human beings.
- They are very cautious about money, and they fear losing it because they fear poverty.
- Their thinking often leads them to greed. They ask others for money, and prefer being consumers to being producers.

The Poor's View of the Wealthy

- All the wealthy are very lucky. Most of them are fools, who do not understand anything.
- The wealthy love money more than themselves. They see nothing else; therefore, we should not trust them.
- The wealthy want money for themselves and their children, but do not wish others would be as rich as they are.
- The wealthy do not know how to get money. They are greedy and teach only their children how to get money.
- The wealthy unite with each other and conspire against all.
- Many wealthy people rob others and harass them, and do not want them to succeed.

The Rich's View of the Poor

- The poor do not deserve money. If they do, then they should learn how to bring it.
- The poor do not appreciate money because they squander it, hoard it, or deal with it badly.
- When the poor get money, they lose it quickly; as they are not ready for it, and they do not develop themselves to learn how to keep it.
- If the rich give the poor all what they have, then they will waste all

fortunes, because they do not know how to invest, just as they are

good at spending and consumption.

- The poor despise money because they cannot get it; therefore, they curse it.
- The poor hate the rich, and hate anyone who owns money, and even hate themselves only because they own that money.

Wealthy people and those who own money constitute 4% – 10% of human beings, but this 10% gradually diminishes, or they are the ordinary rich people. The real wealthy are often those who contribute to the industry of other wealthy people, and those constitute a percentage that does not exceed 4% of all human beings. The poor or those belonging to them, or name them as you like, are the majority of people, who are up to 96%.

You should note that if you look at the rich as bad people; if you laugh at them; if you hate, them, then you will never become like them, just because your mind does not accept this kind of people and how they live. It is surprising that this view of the poor is adopted toward the rich as if the rich are those who have deprived them of having fortunes and made them poor. Finally, if money were a human that had feelings, then how would it react to each of them? What is his view of them, whether towards those who do not have money like the poor or those who own money like the rich?

Now, and after having clarified the views of the rich and the poor toward each other, as well as their view of money- then what is your view of each of them? What is your view of money?

It is your thoughts that make up your inner and outer world. You, your life, your financial success, and your fortune are the only results of your thoughts, that cause your poverty or your wealth. By changing your convictions and ideas, and developing yourself and investing in your mind, then your life will change completely, and your wealth will grow. Wealthy people can simply recover their money and fortune if they lose it because they are the ones who lead and control it, while the poor cannot. Their habits and behaviors are radically different and

disproportionate to wealth and abundance. The wealthy have a greater mindset than the problems and challenges they encounter. They love to learn from those who are better than they. They believe that everything is possible, and they always adopt a positive attitude toward money.

We should now think about the following:

Is money important?
Yes, it is important.
Is money a blessing?
Yes, it is a blessing.
Do we believe in the importance of having a fortune?
Yes, we believe in the importance of being rich.
Is money worthy of love?
Yes, money is worthy of love.

It is not for those who think of those ideas to destroy what they have built to start rebuilding fortunes again. One does not have to stop making money if he works for it. All he has to do is to achieve his goals through money, and start thinking about how to convert money to work for him, not the other way around. First of all, you have to change your mindset toward money, then gain the skill necessary for that, and you have to make a quick decision to free yourself from the money complex. If you look at money, it will flow to you from several sources. You have to look for the best source that does not concern you much.

Sources of money flow

Money flows from many sources. It does not discriminate persons when it chooses them. The source is not the one that chooses them. Some people spend all their time working for money, but get limited money, while others work for some time for money, and make more money than their peers. The amount of money is not related to the amount of time spent on it. There are people who work hard, do hard

work to get money, while others do less hard work, make less effort, and make more money. The amount of money is not related to the amount of effort made for it.

On the other hand, there are people who do nothing and do not make any effort or spend any of their time for money, but they make more money than others. Therefore, getting money and spending it is not related to the two factors of "effort and time". There are also intelligent people who do not have money, and there are others who are less intelligent, but have more money. Therefore, intelligence has nothing to do with how much money we get.

If we think a little about the minds of the poor, we will find that they do their best to make money, which, in turn, turns into expenses to meet the demands of life. As long as they want money, they have to continue to spend time and effort. If one only saves money for the sake of saving itself, without investing it, then money will remain static until this person puts his hand on it again and turns it into, for example, traveling expenses or buying a car. Then one should continue to exert additional effort and time to get more money. The more expenses and prices go up, the more effort and time are spent.

On the contrary, those who have the mindset of the wealthy, they spend their time and effort not only for money, but they work hard to obtain assets that generate money for them so that their efforts and time are gradually reduced and their money keeps increasing. Assets begin to operate on their own, and they give their owner money forever.

To clarify more, in the first case, i.e., those who have the mindset of the poor, the rule is as follows:

First operation (1)	The current result (2)	Final result (3)
Exerted effort + Time spent	Money which= turns into expenses	Continuing to work for money forever

Here the person draws his energy and his time to get money. Therefore, he spends more than 60% of his time for money that sooner or later turns into expenses. The more money he wants to spend, the more time he needs to spend and the more energy he needs to exert to increase money, because he earns money in return for time and energy. This rule falls under the rubric 'labor with effort'.

In the second case, i.e., those who have the mindset of the wealthy, the rule is as follows:

First operation (1)	The current result (2)	Final result (3)
Exerted effort + Time spent	=Money to buy assets Then the assets generate money later.	Works for building assets, then assets take care to work for money forever.

In this case, one spends his energy and time to obtain financial assets such as real estate, for example, and this continuously generates money, because after having assets, this will generate money without effort and time. Then he can stop working, making energy and spending time hard for money, because it is his assets that do all the work and without the need for any intervention by him. This rule falls under the rubric 'smart work'.

It is, therefore, necessary for any person seeking wealth to be aware of these two rules, which will help him personally to make money without taking up 60% of his time, so he can get rid of the node of work for money, and can even be liberated from it.

Returning to the sources of money flow, which is divided into several sections, we will find it as follows:

1) Job: It is the first source for those who work in the government sector or the private sector. The idea of this source is that one commits his time and effort to money, and this is "to get a fixed salary". However, if he stops work, his income will stop; thus, it is a risk and will not achieve the principle of "job security." If a person works in a job he loves, and brings him happiness, or a job that provides a great service to his homeland, then he can continue if he should serve his homeland, but at the same time, he should create an additional source of income that depends on assets. This additional source will help him feel more secure, more creative because it is more stable and safer. If a person does not like his job, he must work as quickly as possible to search for other sources based on the assets that generate money.

(2) **Small businesses:** They are the second source which is represented in self-employment as an entrepreneur or as professionals such as engineers, doctors and lawyers. This person has the greater opportunity to open his own business while he does not receive a fixed salary at the end of the month. However, if he stops working, then his income will stop, and here lies the risk again. This risk also applies to a person who depends on the first source, which is only his "job."

(3) **Ownership of companies and projects:** It is the third source which is concerned with the establishment of a system that works.

10

The system works alone and efficiently; as it regulates all employees

and workers in the company, as well as regulates the mechanism of obtaining revenues and sales and calculating expenses. After the system is built and the owner stops working, then income will continue to flow, as it is already generating income, and does not depend on the work of the owner nor his effort and time.

(4) **Investments:** It is the fourth source of financial flow sources. Investment means, for example, a person buys shares in existing companies or real estate that is subsequently leased with a sum of money. Therefore, these investments achieve periodic financial profits and do not depend on the work of the owner nor his efforts and time. Therefore, there is no need to work, but to make profitable and lucrative investments to achieve financial freedom.

To link the two bases, in the two tables reviewed, with regard to explaining the difference between the mindset of the wealthy and their intelligent work, and the mindset of the poor and their hard work to make money – and to link them to the four sources from which money flows — we find that there are sources of money flowing through one's activity, and these sources are related to the time he spends, as well as his effort in terms of quantity, while there are sources from which money flows through the assets that generate money, and these are not related to the amount of time of the one who has assets nor related to his effort, but they are related to how he exerts time and effort.

Thus, we notice that most people are the source of their income, and the flow of money to them emerges through their jobs and small businesses, while few people have income through their ownership of assets. It is possible to name the two sources, the first and the second, as 'traditional sources,' because most people rely on them, while the third and fourth sources can be named as non-traditional sources.

First: Traditional Sources

The "traditional source" of financial attainment is that a person works a job of a specific type to earn for his day's sustenance, and because he

has established in his mind that his livelihood is linked to his work, he drains most of his energy and time, as well as concentration in favor of production in that job, lest he loses his gains from his job in case he fails in it. If someone does not have a job, then he should try to adopt a personal idea to launch his own business.

The production of his project from inside his house may be within private possessions owned by him; in fact, these possessions are not guaranteed by profits, and they are unstable. In better cases, one tends to establish his own business, who may initially be able to launch that project, but soon he will realize that he is demanded to continue working continuously to keep the wheel of financial gain in circulation; thus, if he stops, then his earnings will stop, because these earnings require continuous work to ensure that consumers, from whom he can earn financial income, will be attracted.

More than 95% of the people earn their financial income from the "traditional source" of financial attainment. The vast majority go to this type of income believing that ideal opportunities require considerable capital and good fortune, while they do not believe that too many people could move from the "traditional source" to investing in financial assets, just because the latter believed they could do it; thus, worked for that.

The transition to investment in assets, a constant income, remains a dream for all those who work under the umbrella of jobs and small projects that provide the "traditional source," which makes money for their owners. Those remain under the pressure of work and the inevitability of making the greatest effort for the more abundant harvest. Therefore, they are occupied with this idea throughout their lives and until their retirement or death.

Second: Non-traditional Sources

Only 5% of the people have been able to build, maintain and develop these sources of financial attainment. The source of financial assets is

considered within the continuous income for their owners. It is a steady and growing income. At the time those of 'non-traditional source' work to make their money, and work within these assets owned by the other class of people who own commercial agencies and real estate, and who have shares in major companies on the stock market — those who own that definitely enjoy mental comfort, because they control their time as they wish. Therefore, it comes clear to us the importance that anyone desiring wealth has to be aware of the sources that generate money; thus, he has to seek freedom from the work node for the sake of money, and he should tend to build assets.

Optimal Handling of Money

The solution is to achieve opulence and wealth in building a true relationship with money through the correct belief and outlook toward its flow. The solution is also to obtain an asset and an investment of money through the optimal handling of that money.

The movement of money in all joints of life is as follows:

- Money entering your own treasury from an external source is called revenue.
- Money coming out of your personal treasury to any place other than investment is called an expense.

If you have money that is saved, then any income that comes to your wallet stays in it, but it either turns into an expense, or it remains saved. With the aging of time, it becomes less than its actual value, or it turns into an asset that generates other money and becomes income.

It is natural that the process of transferring money to expenses is not the best deal with money, while keeping money saved is better than spending it, and saving money for saving in itself leads to increasing it until its fate is determined between being converted into expenses or being stored and devalued — or being invested and replaced with assets. Although it is important to save money, the most important thing is the fate of this saving, because it will soon be exhausted, unless there is a renewable resource that continually fills your money wallet.

Here we can ask ourselves the most important question: how can we deal optimally with money, as well as achieve and build the source or origin that generates money continuously and growingly which will help us gain wealth?

In the following chapter, we will take you, dear reader, to an exciting and amazing journey accompanied by a number of characters who were selected after careful research. They are the most prominent in the world in achieving amazing success and wealth, culminating their lives full of lessons and good examples based on scientific evidence. These will inspire you that will, hopefully, lead you to the process of building real wealth. Wealth does not necessarily mean access to large amounts of money, but it also means, to obtain a high level of success through which these characters could achieve their hopes and aspirations in steady and studied steps.

We will be, through the following chapters, indulging in the inspirational biographies of rich emperors based on scientific sources and evidence. Together, we will learn about their lives from the beginning until their achievement of that wealth, and how they were able to translate all their attitudes of life into indicators that helped them directly to be on the throne of the wealthiest people of the world. We will review with you in those exciting chapters how their view of money was; the mechanism of earning money and increasing it; what they did to achieve that; and how they were able to employ every opportunity experienced in the sources of the flow of money until money began to work for them rather than they work for it.

Warren Buffett
"The Foreteller of Stock Market"

2

Warren Buffett, The Foreteller of Stock Market

Childhood and Family

Warren Buffett was born in 1930 in Nebraska, USA, during the great depression that followed World War I. He spent his childhood, with his two sisters, under the care of his parents. His father worked as an employee at the Stock Trading Office, but was fired a year after his birth. Then, he started his own project of money trading in a small office using his savings.

Warren Buffett's mother took good care of her children, but she was harsh in dealing with them. When she was angry, especially when she suffered from chronic headaches, she would beat them. This created fear and dread for those who were around her.

Warren spent most of his time in his father's office that provided him with much information in stock trading. His father always instilled self-confidence and responsibility in him, and allowed him to work. Warren worked as a soft drink and chewing gum salesman.

Education

Warren Buffett was fond of reading since he was young, spending hours reading at his father's office. The first book he read at seven years old was on investment. To this day, he still spends five to six hours a day reading.

Warren's father won a seat in the US Senate, forcing the family to move to Washington, which made Warren lose interest in school. He became mischievous, and he underachieved academically. Once, he pranked on his teachers at school, who were investing their pension in AT & T. He told them that he sold ten shares of the company in the form of short selling, indicating that the price of the stock was going down. This created panic among his teachers.

Warren Buffett felt that he had disappointed his father, so he worked to improve his academic performance. Warren was not interested in college because he was investing in stocks and renting Ben Paul games inside entertainment centers. At the same time, he distributed newspapers, but his father pushed him to complete his studies.

Warren Buffett enrolled at the University of Pennsylvania, where he studied for two years. Then he moved to Nebraska to complete his college. He was a business administration student. He continued his studies in higher education, where he joined Columbia University after corresponding to Benjamin Graham, an author in the investment books he read. This author lectured at this university, and his influence was very strong on Warren's practical life.

The Beginning of Work

After graduating from the University of Columbia, Warren Buffett began setting up a trading company. Some of his relatives shared $105,100, while Warren paid $100 of that amount. He did everything in the first six years. During this period, he dealt with small companies that were about to be bankrupt, so that he could take advantage of the last profits.

After six years, the company owned nearly $7 million in investment. In 1962, Warren Buffett began buying shares in Berkshire Hathaway, which was investing in spinning and weaving plants but was heading for a loss. As a result, it closed many of its businesses. Two years later, Warren held a deal with Berkshire Hathaway to buy his own shares at $11.5 per share, but later found out that the contract was written at $11.375 per share. This infuriated him. He decided to buy most of the company shares, which consequently made him control and change the company's board of directors. He ran the company until 1967 when the investments in the insurance sector had expanded. This helped the company grow.

Social Life

The American billionaire, Bill Gates, has been the close, personal friend of Warren Buffett since 1991, and both have shared each other numerous political and charitable projects. They have been guiding and directing each other. Warren gets up every morning, goes to work, and buys breakfast from McDonald's along the way, while his wife puts money in the car purse based on the stock market situation of the day. If his share price is low, he buys a low-cost breakfast, if it is not, then he buys the expensive meal. In the evening, when he returns home, he spends some time with his children, and takes time to read.

Staff

Warren Buffett knew Charlie Manager at a lunch where he was invited to be an investor. Charlie was a lawyer who had a lot of influence on Warren on investments by taking advantage of the latest profits through investment in assets and companies of good management.

Warren Buffett has a huge staff at Berkshire Hathaway, but he deals with only 25 of them in a small office in Omaha, the company's headquarters. The office has kept its shape and staff for more than

50 years. Warren follows rule number one, which he learned from his teacher Benjamin Abraham: Whatever you do, you should not lose

the money you have invested, and it is advisable to focus on what you love and identify your circle of interests and not to worry about what happens outside. You have to wait for the right time to invest, and do not make greed and temptations lead you to invest, and do not make feelings affect your decisions.

Painful Past

Warren Buffett was upset when his family decided to move from Nebraska to Washington after his father had won a seat in the US Congress. This move caused loss of his friends, in addition to what he has suffered from his mother's cruelty, and his father's preoccupation with other things over him. This led him to flee their house, but it was a failed attempt as a police patrol grabbed him and returned him to his house. The strange thing was that his father did not get angry, rather told him: "You can do better than that." Warren felt that his father was disappointed, which pushed him to be diligent and resolved in school and at work.

Challenges

One of Warren Buffett's main challenges in his career was the crisis with Salomon Brothers Bank. Warren was critical of the investment banks. However, despite his dissatisfaction with the environment in which these banks operate, he invested in them. Shortly after Warren's entry into investment banks, something unexpected happened. Salomon Brothers Bank was accused of illegal trading in the treasury bonds of the State, exceeding the maximum trading limit and buying bonds for customers without their knowledge. As a result of these accusations, customer trust in investment banks has wavered, as well as the trust of other countries in the US market. Warren's reputation was at stake,

and he had 24 hours to make a decision, either to declare the bank bankrupt or to take full responsibility and try to fix it. Warren took a courageous step by taking full responsibility of managing the bank. He tried to convince the US government that what the bank did was stupid, and that he would do his best to reform it; that bankruptcy could destroy a large part of the US stock exchange. Indeed, Warren's good reputation has helped him overcome this crisis. That reputation he built through his previous dealings has made the US government trust him in reforming it.

Passion

Warren Buffett had a special relationship with numbers and accounts. He was a genius, and he has inherited this aptitude from his mother. Warren took advantage of this gift, and used it in the field of investment. He was quick in analyzing corporate stock reports and selecting successful stocks.

Dream And Goal

Warren Buffett's goal was to have a lot of money, and become rich. He had this dream ever since he was young and told his sister that he would become a millionaire at 30 years old. He had already achieved so, as his fortune amounted to $1 million in 1960. This dream evolved as he dreamed of being the richest man in the world.

Turning Point

When Warren Buffett was 21, he married Susan Tomson, a 19-year-old, in 1952. Her presence in his life created a very high balance. She was the friendly person he did not find in his mother. She gave him great care that made him extremely focused on his work. Their marriage created a turning point becoming interested in civil rights and freedoms.

Persistence and Continuity

Warren Buffett did not allow the challenges he faced to reverse his goals. He was rejected by the Harvard School of Business after graduating from Nebraska University. In a short interview with the person who was responsible for admission at Harvard College, he told him: "You have to forget it. You will not go to Harvard." That rejection was a big disappointment to Warren Buffett. He discovered that his top models, Benjamin Graham and David Dodd, were professors at Columbia Business School. This led him to send a letter to them: "Dear Professors, Dodd and David.....I thought you were dead, but now I have discovered that you are alive and teaching at the University of Columbia. I really want to study at this university." After that speech, Warren Buffett was accepted to enroll at the University of Columbia.

The series of frustrations that Warren encountered in his life continued, but this did not stop him; rather, challenged him to increase his tenacity and perseverance to achieve his dream. When he proposed to his wife in 1951, her father requested for a meeting on the subject. He found out later that his father-in-law did not have much confidence in Warren's plans, and the former insisted that Warren would face failure, and his daughter would suffer from hunger because he would inevitably fail. This was what her father expected.

Success

Warren Buffett has achieved many successes in his life, and these successes are attributed to three people:

The first is his father, Howard Buffett, whom he considers his superhero, and one of his most important teachers. One of the most important lessons he learned from him is good reputation is more important than money. This helped Warren overcome the Salomon Brothers Bank crisis of the nineties. It was his good reputation that the

US government allowed him to run the investment bank.

The second person is his wife, Susan Thompson, who helped stabilize his life, and helped him focus on success.

The last person is his professor, Benjamin Abraham, from whom he learned the rules of investment and the cloning of the successful persons. These rules formed the bases of Warren's success.

Warren Buffett's first success was when he managed to invest the $105,000 he set up in his office for trading, which became nearly $7 million in just seven years. This was followed by the acquisition of Berkshire Hathaway, which currently includes all Warren Buffett investments.

Warren Buffett was named as the legend of wealth. He has the best records of ingenuity in the face of market volatility; so that people would pay millions of dollars just to have lunch with him. He has collected nearly $20 million for a luncheon that he donated the proceeds to charity.

One of the most important tips Warren gives to investors is that they have to clone the successful persons, one of the rules taught by Benjamin Abraham. All you have to do to succeed in investing is to do what those successful people do and enjoy what you do. One should not let life go without doing what he wants. He has to surround himself with those who share his thoughts and make his own decisions without letting other people drive his vehicle. He has to determine his circle of abilities and interests. This is the circle in which he will succeed in competing.

Funding

When his family moved to Nebraska, Warren Buffett distributed the Washington Post newspapers every morning, earning about $157 a month, more than the salary most teachers received at that time. He also did many side jobs such as selling golf balls and selling stamps to amateur collectors, as well as doing car polishing.

By the 16th year, Warren Buffett had raised $53,000, and by 2013 his income had increased to $17 million a day. His fortune at the time was estimated at $59 billion, up from $46 billion at the beginning of the same year.

On average, Warren Buffett collected nearly $37 million a day, with more than 94% of his wealth collected after he turned 60 years old.

Giving

Warren Buffett was at odds with his wife, Suzanne, regarding giving. Suzanne was helpful and generous in giving, and always thought she would marry someone who would serve the community; such as marrying a doctor or an engineer, but she noted that Warren was investing money to make more money and give nothing to the community. Warren Buffett's view was that what he does that which can be done by anyone and the information he has is available to everyone. All they have to do is to make an effort. This prompted Susan to move away from Warren in her late life as she was fully engaged in philanthropy. In 2000, Warren Buffett held a charity fundraising event to fight poverty. Nearly $3.4 million was raised. In 2006, Warren donated 85% of his earnings from Berkshire Hathaway to charitable organizations, including Gates Foundation, owned by his friend, Bill Gates, as this share is dispensed as gifts every year.

Lifestyle now

Warren Buffett is a sugar enthusiast. Coca-Cola and Dairy Queen are among his most significant investments. He is known to eat like a six-year-old child, has a daily breakfast from McDonald's, and drinks five to six Coca-Cola daily. Warren Buffett's medical examination showed that he had prostate cancer, which was found in his periodic health check every six months. He was fortunate enough to overcome his illness after undergoing radiotherapy for five months. Warren Buffett is the third richest man and the wealthiest investor in the world. He is

one of the most well-known wealthy, with a fortune of $84 billion. By 2018, Warren had entered the world of wealth when he was 30. When he got his first million after nearly 10 years of setting up his small trading office. Then, He was able to continue to grow until his fortune reached $1 billion in 1986. He was classified as the world's richest man in 2008.

Richard Branson
"The Rebel Billionaire"

3

Richard Branson, The Rebel Billionaire

Childhood and Family

Richard Branson was born on July 18, 1950, and was the first child of a lawyer, Edward Branson, and Eve, his mother. Richard Branson grew up in a family of adventure and achievement, as Edward's mother wanted him to be an archaeologist, but his father wanted him to follow the family tradition, which was to join law school. Richard obeyed his father's will and practised law. However, this did not prevent him from owning his own collection of antiques and fossils. When World War II broke out in 1939, Edward joined the cavalry regiment to volunteer in war.

Eve Branson was a benefactor and an entrepreneur with a strong personality. She had her own adventures when she wanted to be a pilot. She tried to join the Flight Club, and when she was rejected because of her sex, she managed to convince one of the supervisors to get the job disguised as a man. After the war, she served as a flight attendant.

Richard Branson's childhood was the cornerstone of his success. His family supported him with, challenge, rigor, understanding and love. Richard Branson recalls a remarkable story in his childhood when his mother woke him up before the sunrise, and asked him to go to his relatives' home in Bournemouth, 50 miles away. She provided him

with some sandwiches, but did not provide him with water. She asked him to find water for himself. At that time, Richard was pushing 12 years old. His mother wanted to develop his stamina and develop his sense of direction. Richard embarked on the journey and spent the night in his relatives' house. When he returned home, he was proud of this great achievement. His mother greeted him with admiration, and asked him if he had enjoyed the trip. Richard's parents always make their children feel their love, and appreciate everyone's opinions.

Education

In his youth, Richard suffered from dyslexia. For him, it was a great challenge in his school life. He abandoned his studies at the age of 16, but Richard saw life as a lifelong learning process, and not limited to school life. He never stopped learning. He saw in every project he has created that he needs to learn new skills and acquire new pieces of information. He just could not succeed in a new project, relying only on his experiences. Success depends on the skill of listening, as his awareness of his lack of knowledge makes him take care of others' advice and experience.

The Beginning of Work

Richard Branson was fond of the idea of building his own project, as influenced by his mother. Richard tried several attempts to start his own business. He and his friend, Nik, tried planting and selling Christmas trees and selling birds, but these two attempts did not work out. Together with his friend John James, He created "Student," a magazine dedicated to campaigning against corporal punishments on unproductive students. Richard came up with a deeper idea of the project. He wanted to publish it at the school level, and share it with other schools. He faced many challenges in his attempt to issue the maiden issue of the magazine, especially the cost of printing. To finance his project, he sent out many letters to prospective sponsors explaining the objectives of the magazine and its role in supporting youth. Unfortunately, he did not receive any response from most of those he had addressed to. The responses were mostly letters of encouragement and moral support. The work of "Richard" focused on administrative matters, and their work station was a room in the basement of the home of his partner, John James.

Richard Branson was not able to publish the maiden issue of the magazine until he sold advertising spaces to nine large companies that agreed to buy. The sale of advertising space has always been the bone of contention in this project. He was able to issue the first edition of the magazine in 1968, one year after, and surprisingly, the manager of his school sent him a congratulatory letter on the publication of the magazine's maiden issue.

In the fall of 1968, Richard was forced to look for another place to live and work, as the parents of his partner, John, did not feel comfortable with the noise in their basement. They asked John to complete his university studies, instead of wasting his time in the magazine. With John gone, he asked his friend Nick Paul to join the magazine. He was a wonderful addition to the team, as he organized tasks, managed expenses, as well as administered affairs more professionally.

Richard and his colleagues faced a major problem in finding a place to work in the magazine. One of their supporters offered them to work for free in a church cemetery. They moved over as they had no options. For a short period of time, the cemetery served as their publication office and workstation.

Richard paid the magazine staff 20 pounds a week. However, what struck his attention was that some of his employees would rather buy versions of the latest music albums over food and clothing. Richard thought of beginning a new project: selling records and songs by mail, which later evolved to become Virgin Records Series. That was the beginning of Virgin Group, the big brand.

Social Life

Richard Branson is by nature a well-liked personality. He has a great ability to win friends, making him always surrounded by people who form a loving and harmonious environment.

Richard wakes up at five in the morning every day. Then, he spends an hour or more, reading his e-mail, replying to a number of messages, reading international news, and then walk, run, or go to the sports club. He spends some time playing tennis or skiing on Necker Island if the weather is fine. After his physical workout, Richard takes his breakfast with his family, and goes to work.

Staff

Richard has always said that daily work should be fun. He is one of the biggest supporters of home-based work and flexible time. In an interview regarding his dyslexia and its impact on his success, he said that his situation may be one of the most important reasons for his success, as his inability to master the requirements of work made him seek the help of those who are better. That's why, Virgin Group today has more than 60,000 employees. When Richard Branson bought Necker Island, he made it a perfect place to stay out of the world and spend enough time for himself and his family. "When you're deep in the event, it's hard for you to find a solution to the problems, but when you are outside the event, you can see clearly, making it easier to find solutions."

Richard has a unique way of winning the love of his staff; he appreciates what they are doing and considers them his own close friends. He likes to share them all occasions, whether on the professional level or on the personal and social levels. He always advises entrepreneurs to protect their employees. He confirms that the employer's perception that he is their source of income should make him fight more vigorously for success and refuse to surrender.

Painful Pas

Richard Branson's suffering from dyslexia was not the only challenge he suffered. He was also so poor in sight that he could not read what was written on the board even if he was at the front seats of his class.

Because the teachers at that time were not aware of the reality of dyslexia, they believed that those who experienced such difficulties were either lazy or stupid, and the penalty for both cases was either beating or the writing of homework several times. Therefore, Richard had become convinced that he would be punished by beating twice, at least, a week. Because of his failure in most subjects, Richard's parents decided to transfer him to a private school, but he did not miss punishment and continued to suffer beatings and reprimands there, too. Richard abandoned his study in 1967, when he was 16, and began his career. He mentioned in one of his books that the headmaster told him on the day of his departure, "You will either end up in prison, or you'll become a millionaire someday."

When Richard Branson was asked how he succeeded in persuading his parents to leave school, he said: "That matter took three rounds around the house with my father. In the first round, my father answered quietly, "You really have to try to finish your education." In the second round when I told my father that I had taken the decision to leave my study, then he began to be lenient with me. In the third round, he said to me, 'Do you know? When I was 23 years old, I did not know what I wanted to do. You know, at least, what you want to do.' My parents understood my situation, and I think what helped them was the fact that I was a hopeless case in school."

Challenges

The suffering of Richard Branson from dyslexia during his childhood made his education difficult, but looking back, he knew he had high mathematical aptitude, especially in the form of money. This gave him

the idea on how to overcome hardship in reading, selling and buying. It made it easier for him to focus, and applied that on messages, letters, and other texts. He mentioned in one interview that dyslexia was an element of his success. That made him focus entirely on what he was good at, and he deputized others to do the work he could not do. This made him good at deputizing the right people to do different tasks. He also said that by the time he was 50, he could not differentiate between net profit and total income, until one of the managers compared it to the net and fish, making things clearer and understandable to him.

One of the most impressive experiences of Richard was when he was invited to participate in a speech on human rights in his capacity as the founder of Student Magazine. It was at the College of London University, where among those invited were the political activist and journalist, Tariq Ali, and the leader of the student movement in Germany, the politician Daniel Cohen Bendt. Both gave an enthusiastic and inspiring speech. Richard mentioned that he was impressed by their speeches. When his turn came, he was bewildered. He remembered when he was at school, students had to give a speech to everyone, and when a student made a mistake or was in confusion, the teacher immediately stopped that student and prevented him from completing his speech. The result would be students booed. That bad experience he did not want to remember made him feel tired before giving his speech. When he wanted to give his speech, he found himself overwhelmed by uncontrollable fear and fatigue that made him leave that place.

Passion

Richard Branson often attributes his success to his ability to deputize others to do what they know. He sees deputizing as a skill that every entrepreneur needs to succeed, and that it is difficult to get out of the high pressures at work without deputizing. When Richard deputized his friend Nick to manage Student Magazine, Nick managed to organize

work and cut expenses. When he added Simon to the team of Virgin Record, he managed, with his help, the Virgin Records properly. Simon had high skill in selecting bands. He also deputized David Tate, who led Virgin Atlantic with great success.

Dream and Goal

Richard Branson recalls the days after his 40th birthday, Vanity Fair Magazine interviewed him. When he was asked about his dreams and goals, he found himself actualized everything he wanted. He has proven his worth for himself, and achieved enough accomplishments and victories, which made him decide to stop expanding. He sold all his investments, be satisfied with Virgin Atlantic, which he loved so much. Almost a month later, the Gulf War and the Iraqi invasion of Kuwait broke out. When coalition forces decided to bomb Iraq, former Iraqi President Saddam Hussein appeared on television and announced the use of some foreign prisoners as human shields if coalition forces attacked. Richard Branson recalled that the appearance of the Iraqi president, along with a child of the captives, motivated his fatherhood to try to save his captives. The negotiations were conducted by King Hussein of Jordan. With the success of the negotiations, Richard Branson managed to find the real goal for all of his actions. While some newspapers were praising the courage and wisdom of Richard in dealing with the situation, other newspapers were attacking his work because of his intervention in political action and his attempt to gain popularity politically. However, he defended what he did and told the media that what prompted him to do so was his love to help. He could not accept to remain idle, as he had the ability to participate positively. We can see the truthfulness of what he said in all of his investments. He published the Student Magazine with the idea of correcting and developing schools, and solving the problems of students and adolescents. His establishment of Virgin Records was also an attempt to create a place where customers would feel satisfied

with the music records, not available in big stores. We can see the truthfulness of his speech about his Virgin Atlantic, whose idea came with the problem of canceling its flight. He focused on organizing flights to places that were not provided by other airlines. His airline was the first to provide onboard entertainment. His Virgin Mobile for communications was founded to provide the best offers at prices that would suit everyone, in general, and suit young people, in particular. He was the engine of real success, and his ultimate goal was to help others.

The Turning Point

It was one of the most important turning points for Richard Branson when he was jailed for tax evasion in 1971. He had to hand over an order to Belgium. He received some cassettes and tried to transfer them to Belgium, but he forgot some papers and the authorities prevented him from crossing the French borders and forced him to return. Then, he discovered the truth of his acquisition of this amount of cassettes that he did not pay the tax for, and that would save him the cost of the tax, in the case of sale. Through a simple calculation, he could estimate that three operations of this kind will be enough to pay all his debts, as he had taken a loan, by which he bought a house in a suburb and turned it into a company to record albums. He also borrowed an amount from his aunt, who mortgaged her house, to ensure it for him. He also had the amount saved by his parents for the time of distress. That was tempting for him, that he repeated this operation three times as he did not expect anyone to try to do the same process, and perhaps, in more intelligent and sophisticated ways. One night he received a call from an unknown person, telling him that the inspectors will inspect the place, and telling him that they knew what he was doing. When he asked him why he had helped him, he said that Richard had helped one of his friends when he was trying to commit suicide and made him abandon his decision. That night, Richard and his partners collected all the cassettes and moved them to the other store, as he did not expect them to inspect all the stores. After the matter was revealed, he was arrested the night before the trial. According to him, it was the finest night in his life. He reckoned that he had spent his life before that night indifferent to laws, living the life of absolute freedom without punishment. That night, however, he felt that he had been deprived of his liberty, and the first expectation of the headmaster of his school came true, when he told him before leaving school, "I expect either you will go to prison or you will become a millionaire." He also remembered the advice of his father when he told him, "You can live happilly even if you lose all your money, but you will lose everything if you lose your reputation."

That night, Richard felt he was being held accountable for his actions. He promised himself that he would not do anything that might harm his reputation again. In court, he told the judge that he did not have the required bail, but his mother, who was present, told the judge that she was willing to mortgage the family farm for a bail on Richard's release. This made him feel that he had not lost his family's trust. His mother also told him when he went out that everyone makes mistakes and that he only had to learn from his mistakes.

This was not only a turning point, it was also the turning point for his partners as they began to work harder and took firm actions. Their sole aim was to repay Richard's debts and ensure he would not be re-incarcerated. As a result, and after settling with the Tax Department, which amounted to three times the value of the tax, in return for not completing the trial — Richard opened approximately 24 new stores within two years at the rate of one store per month. Within three years, he managed to repay all his debts; yet he still could make a fortune.

Persistence and Continuity

The family of Richard Branson sought to prepare him to be a stubborn and adventurous entrepreneur, as they saw that as the basis for the

challenges of life. At the age of five, Richard was on a trip with his family to the beach. His aunt, Joyce, challenged him, so she ran into a tiny amount of money that he would not learn to swim in two weeks. This bet was a real motivation for his challenging of waves and for continuing until late with the cold water at night. The two weeks went by, he still did not know how to swim, so his parents and his aunt comforted him for that loss. During the trip, Richard looked out of the car window to see the course of a nearby river. Richard wanted to make a final attempt. He asked his parents to stop to try again. He went quickly to the river for fear that his parents would change their mind. When he jumped into the river, he found swimming in it was less complicated than the sea and its waves. He managed to swim on that day and win the bet of his aunt. He also mentioned that his father could not control himself because he was very proud of him, that his father also jumped into the river and hugged him. Everyone applauded him for that achievement, and this was the seed of persistence that made him resist the loss in a number of his works.

Success

Richard Branson defines success as 'making a change for the better in life, in general,' and he firmly believes that success is not just by looking for money. We know that Student Magazine cared about discussing the problems and concerns of young people, as it participated in representing young people in demonstrations against the Vietnam War and other political events. Moreover, his Virgin Records has provided young people with fun and music, and Virgin Atlantic had provided convenient flights and has become the first company to provide inflight entertainment for travelers. The success of Richard led Queen Elizabeth II to honor him for his entrepreneurial achievements, on December 30, 1999. He also obtained the rank of "Sir" on 30 March. He was honored by Prince Charles, the Prince of Wales and the eldest son of the Queen. To this day, Richard Branson, together with Virgin Galactic, does the

research necessary to provide tourism trips to space.

There are lots of advice put forward by Richard Branson to help young people in many areas. He mentioned in one of his books that the best advice he got was from his mother: "One should not waste time in regret, but one should go ahead." Richard is surprised by the amount of time people spend on decisions that cannot be corrected, and his mother always warned him against undervaluing others or underestimating them. She punished him if he erred, by making him stand five minutes to see himself in the mirror, indicating to him that devaluing others devalues himself.

Funding

The most challenging thing for entrepreneurs is their need for sufficient capital to start their own business, and people are often afraid of loans and debt. Richard Branson, in his advice to entrepreneurs, says it is impossible to succeed in any real project without risk. As long as an entrepreneur believes in the idea, all he has to master is to display it properly and to go to those who can help.

Giving

The journey of giving began early in his career, long before he was over 20 years old. He had a transient relationship with a girl, named Debbie, who told him one day, she had signs of pregnancy and that she had decided to undergo an abortion. Richard and Debbie went to public hospitals, but their request was rejected. The policy of public hospitals stated that pregnancy should not be miscarried unless the pregnancy is a threat to the mother's life, which led them to resort to private clinics. Richard recalls that the cost of the operation was 400 pounds, and they did not have the money at that time. After a long search, one female doctor offered to help him with only 50 pounds, and the operation was successful. Richard Branson's attention was drawn by the tremendous

effort he made to reach this doctor and the suffering of adolescents in solving their problems, especially the problems they cannot explain to their parents.

As a result, Richard decided to start a charity project under the name, *"Give Us A Headache That Is Within You."* Richard has created a wide network of adolescent specialists and doctors, some of whom have offered discounts to adolescents, and in some cases, granted free treatment and counseling, which has helped resolve many of the issues of depression and suicide attempts by teenagers. The name of this project turned later into "Help!", and today it is part of the Virgin Unite team, which manages such many charitable projects as protecting marine life, supporting clean energy, confronting global warming, supporting emerging projects, fighting drugs, fighting famine and rescuing disaster areas. Richard Branson has also created a prize to address environmental challenges. The award presents the best proposals for addressing environmental challenges and saving the earth from pollution.

Lifestyle now

Richard Branson created Virgin Music, starting with contracting with young artists and publishing their songs. In 1973, Virgin recorded a distinctive song of the English artist, Mike Oldfield, but it was difficult to persuade the broadcasters to present it until Richard convinced one of the presenters of radio programs to visit him. In Richard's house, the radio presenter listened to the music, and was persuaded to air it over the radio. As a result, he allocated a full episode for the presentation of the song. The radio attracted a large number of customers, and Virgin achieved huge profits at that time, as sales exceeded five hundred million pounds. It was a leap in the life of Richard Branson, through which he was able to enter the world of wealth, where he was then twenty-three years old.

By 2018, Virgin Group, founded by Richard Branson, has 61 active organizations covering more than 53 million customers, employing 69,000 employees and covering 35 countries. This group is valued at $ 22.6 billion, while Richard's wealth exceeded $5 billion. It is already a huge social and commercial empire that Richard Branson dreamed of and worked out to achieve until it became a reality.

Jack Ma
"The Wealth Dragon"

4

Jack Ma, the Wealth Dragon

Childhood and Family

J ack Ma was born on September 10, 1964, in Hangzhou City, southeast of China to a Chinese family of five, including his parents younger brother and sister.

Jack grew up in an impoverished family when China was mostly communist and isolated from the Western world. When he was 12, he used to wake up every morning in a city that had tourism charms. He would then visit the city's central hotels to offer foreign visitors tours in exchange for English lessons, as he was fond of developing his education even at a very young age.

Education

Jack did not have the money and social relations that would help him succeed at the beginning of his life. The only way to succeed was through education. After completing his studies, Jack went to university, but did not pass the entrance examination twice. He finally succeeded on his third attempt at the entrance examination to the Hangzhou College of Teachers.

In 1988, Jack Ma graduated from college with a bachelor's degree in

English. He achieved his ambition by becoming proficient in English with a postgraduate degree in English. He believed English was the most important language in international trade.

The Beginning of Work

After graduating from the university, Jack applied for many jobs, but unfortunately, he was rejected. He applied even for odd jobs, but was still turned down. He even applied for a job in the Kentucky chain of restaurants, but he was also rejected.

Fortunately, Jack Ma got a job as an English teacher at a local university. He said that this language helped him a lot, made him understand the world better, and even felt that he could meet the best officials in the world.

In his first experience as an English teacher, Jack Ma started his job with dedication and enthusiasm. He earned $12 a month.

In 1995, Jack embarked on a trip to the US city of Seattle, where he undertook research on the internet world. The internet was already developed in the United States. From there, he decided to start an internet company, and bring it to his country.

Jack Ma did not have any IT experience. At that time, only a few people in China knew about the internet, or had dealt with it. After three years stint in the US, he returned to China in 1998 to establish an online electronic trading market together with 17 other Chinese. They met to discuss the project and the business strategy. The idea of the online platform would be to allow exporters to display their goods on the internet, enabling customers to buy directly online.

Just one year after that meeting, Jack Ma and his partners launched an online platform called *Alibaba*. The *Alibaba* Group officially started its work in March 1999, and only one year later, in 2000, *Alibaba* got investments of $20 million from investors, such as Softbank, Fidelity, and Golden Sachs.

After two years of lucrative deals with investors, *Alibaba* network was able to get its profits for the first time in 2002. A year later, the network managed to invest $ 450 million to create *Taobao* and *Ali Tok*, which allow buyers to communicate and pay online through *Alibay service*.

In 2004, *Alibaba* received $ 82 million as investments from Softbank, Fidelity and Draper Fisher Jurvetson, becoming the largest private online investment company in China's history. The name of Jack Ma was listed, this year, as one of the top ten leading business characters.

In 2005, Yahoo bought 40% of *Alibaba* network for $ 1 billion. Two years later, the network launched *Ali Mama site* for online marketing. By 2010, *Alibaba* launched *Ali Express service* for export services in China.

Social Life

Jack Ma had a friend named David Morley, whom he met in 1980 during a family trip to China. Since then, he has been a close friend, even one of Jack's best friends, and both had remained close to each other until David's death in 2004.

Jack Ma always loved hard work, looking for new opportunities and adding value to everyone he met in his life. He did not like going home without adding something new to his day, and he was keen to have a better day than yesterday, even if it is a simple change. Jack always remembers his grandfather, who worked for 16 hours every day, while most people work eight hours a day

Like other busy businessmen, Jack Ma spends much of his time flying to many different parts of the world, spending 870 flying hours to meet more than 40 top leaders and decision-makers of governments in many countries to convince them that free trade is good.

Staff

Jack Ma knew that he was very generous and modest with his staff.

He always said that choosing the right person for the job was more important than looking at his talent.

Women account for 47% of *Alibaba*'s total employees, which Jack Ma sees as one of the most important reasons for his organization's success. It gives women plenty of room for work and creativity.

Jack had a distinct theory that he applied to the organization, which is represented in placing customers at the top of the ladder, then employees and finally partners. He said, "I hear what my staff say, but I still do what I see right, but as for customers, I listen to them and follow their advice as much as possible, because a leader must see the best things within each person, through having the skills that make him able to find the strengths in everyone.

In 2013, Jack Ma decided to step down as CEO of *Alibaba* and then Jonathan took over.

Painful Past

Jack Ma has faced a lot of rejection during his life. He failed twice in university admission exams. During the 2016 Economic Forum, he revealed that he was rejected by Harvard University 10 times. When KFC offered 24 jobs, hired 23 except him, his motivation for the challenge to continue and achieve success soared high. He was not dampened by all the rejections he got.

Challenges

Jack Ma named *Alibaba* the *Company With 1001 Mistakes*. He says, "In the first week of the launch of the network, I had only seven employees. They were buying and selling to and from themselves in the network. In the second week of work, customers started selling on the website, and bought everything that was offered for sale by the customers. Most of these things were basically useless, and they did so within the first two weeks of launching their project to tell people that e-commerce is effective and working."

"There were, as many customers do, those who use our site for free.

We did not know how to get money at first," says Jack. "A product of China's exporters was developed to suit American buyers through the online purchase." Jack Ma expresses this system as having saved them. At the end of 2002, he had earned a profit of only one dollar, and every year he sees the evolution. Today, AliBaba's profits keep soaring.

"The day I do not wish to see is the day I retire, and I see the company go down or lose, and this thing I do not want to see because all of us will get sick; all of us will grow up; and all of us will die someday. I do not want to stay at work until I am 70 or 80 years old. I want to die on the beach in the Philippines, not in my office. Nobody wants to see an 80-year-old man who is still the head and working in his office," Jack says.

Passion

Jack Ma is fond of reading and writing, and has many talents and sports interests, especially in martial arts such as Kung Fu and Tai chi. Jack's main interest is meditation. He finds it necessary to have self-reflection every day to satisfy his ambitious and passionate soul.

Jack says he learned English when he was 12 years old. He used to ride his bicycle at five o'clock in the morning for 40 minutes until he came to a hotel to look for tourists to take around the city in exchange for learning English from them.

Dream and Goal

"Success is not just about money, it is about making dreams come true. It is not about the technology that will change the world, it is about our dreams that will change the world," says Jack Ma.

"We aimed to make our customers millionaires. We put them at the beginning of the path, and if they can succeed, *Alibaba* can also succeed after our customers get millions," he said. "We were a major reason to change China in the first 15 years of the 21st century, and we hope in

the next 15 years that the world will change because of us."

With regard to bad ideas, Jack Ma says that he is fine, and one should not be afraid of them, but one must fear that he has no ideas at all.

Jack Ma was not tech-savvy when he was young. Although he runs one of the largest internet companies around the world at this time, he knows nothing more than to send and receive e-mails.

Believing in the importance of each person's talent for achieving what he wants, Jack Ma has launched, through *Alibaba* network, an annual offer for the skills of more than 20,000 employees in his company.

The Turning Point

In 1995, Jack Ma started his project with non-existent material resources, but he saw willpower and teamwork as more important. Many entrepreneurs said he would not build a project without money, but he considers that wrong because entrepreneurship is based on responsibility and teamwork, not money. Money is the last factor in realizing the dream of a successful and global project.

Jack says he once invited 24 people to his residence to explain what he would do with his planned project through the internet. Two hours later, 23 of them told him to forget the idea because it was useless, especially Jack knew nothing about the computer at that time, so how can he invest in the sector in which the only way to go about is the computer? Jack Ma, however, responded that he would try it.

Jack spent that night pondering how to implement his idea until he actually decided to implement it. He was well aware that most people had distinct ideas during the night, and when waking up the next day, if they do not make a decision immediately, then the opportunity is lost because they have returned to their normal routine.

Jack Ma was bold in his decisions, and his decision stemmed from his desire to meet the needs of a huge number of Chinese. *Alibaba*'s e-commerce site helped beat eBay in China by mid-2000.

Persistence and continuity

In the beginning, *Alibaba* did not achieve any financial income. It served free until the third year when it became a profitable company. Jack Ma's vision and determination to achieve success made *Alibaba* today one of the most successful internet companies.

Jack always adopted the slogan "Never give up!" He even issued a book with that title. He always advised entrepreneurs not to chase investors because they would run away very quickly. He said, "The success of any entrepreneur in his/her small or medium project comes from working on development through customers."

Jack Ma believes that it is necessary for each person to learn from the mistakes of others, not to avoid mistakes, but to meet the challenges that follow those mistakes with positive attitude, then success will be achieved.

Success

Jack Ma managed to establish eight companies during the first 15 years of the 21st century, and he still owns seven of them because he sold one of them. He says of his companies: "Whenever I start a new company, I liken it to a new baby and this baby will change me, and this baby will change the world."

Jack has achieved remarkable success in all his projects, especially the network, *Alibaba,* as the amount of circulation and transfer of electronic funds has reached, through *Alibay,* to three quarters of a trillion dollars a year, while *Alibaba* Company has achieved $ 150 billion, which is the largest achievement in the history of the New York Stock Exchange.

The real culmination of Jack Ma's success was his ascension to the throne of China's richest man. Jack Ma's fortune amounted to $ 25 billion in 2014. He held a grand ceremony for all his staff, for his achievement. Jack told them, "I hope you will use your wealth to become noble people, people who help others, people who are full of

goodness and happiness." He said, "When your wealth passes a certain limit, then it will not be your funds, it is the funds of the community that were given to you, and you have to take responsibility until you employ it well and correctly." Jack Ma furthered, "It is possible to reproduce the way, by which we founded *Alibaba*, but the team, as well as the wisdom gained from mistakes, cannot be reproduced. It is not even possible to reproduce ideas and trust of customers, and an employer must strive to do it himself."

Jack Ma has achieved his influence, his fame, and his worldliness. His success was consistent, and he learned from every obstacle in his work. In 2013, Jack was ranked the 30th of the world's most influential people, according to Forbes classification. In the following year, he succeeded in leading *Alibaba* to a success estimated at $238.332 billion, an estimate of the total value of the network *Alibaba*. Jack Ma himself was able to achieve a fortune of $21.8 billion, before the end of the same year. Forbes ranked Jack Ma as the 22nd most powerful man in the world. He was the first Chinese man to appear on the cover of Forbes.

One of the most important arguments of "Jack Ma", which had a global impact is that "trade is not like war, because in the war there are two parties, one of which dies and the other survives, while in the trade, the two parties have to survive in order to achieve their goal of that trade which is profit. He who wants to succeed in his trade must give others strength." The following are some of the most important quotes that have translated the power of the business school launched by Jack Ma:

• You cannot achieve success for your organization without having the trilogy of *message, values, and goals,* clear to you.

• Establish a system based on teamwork, not on one or two individuals.

• A salesperson should not think about money, but he must consider how his product can help the success of consumers and be useful to others, then their trust in his goods and his ability to sell them will increase.

• Learn from the experiences you experience better than to assess your intelligence level.

• There is no official in any organization that does not make mistakes, as every successful person must have made mistakes and faced frustrations.

• Never regret your failure. Rather, try not to repeat the same mistakes.

• Competition gives way to improve yourself, and it is not to defeat the opponent in order to win, because there will always be another competitor.

• An entrepreneur must be able to face failure, and not give up.

Funding

Jack Ma did not mention in all his memoirs that he needed a lot of capital to start his first project, *Ali Baba*. He pointed out that those who aspire to start a project and face a financial dilemma, then the field of online commerce does not need capital to start it, even if an e-business owner needs capital, as it will be minimal.

Giving

One of the things that excited Jack Ma was the environment, so he developed his interest when he joined the International Union for Conservation of Nature in 2009 and joined the board of directors of the World Conservation Council in 2010. In 2015, he spoke during Clinton's session of Global Initiative and contributed to the creation of 27,000 nature reserves in China. After Donald Trump was elected President of the United States, the president met with Jack Ma, who announced he would contribute to the creation of a million jobs in the United States.

Lifestyle now

By the end of 2018, Jack Ma's fortune was $ 42.8 billion, according to Forbes. He was considered one of the world's wealthiest people. He is the owner of *Alibaba Group for E-commerce*, one of the most successful internet companies in the world, valued at $ 300 billion. In 2016, *Alibaba* has made a profit of $ 18 billion. From a poor Chinese family, Jack Ma has grown up since he was young, owning a private plane, which is worth $ 49.7 million.

As for the health aspect, Jack continuously indulges in sports, maintaining his health through martial arts training. One of his most important goals is to make people healthier and happier.

Elon Musk
"The Iron Man"

5

Elon Musk, the Iron Man

Childhood and Family

Elon Musk was born on June 28, 1971, in South Africa's Pretoria City. He was known as an introverted child. He did not like to share his thoughts with others, as described by his father, Errol Musk who was working as an electromechanical engineer. His mother, Maye Musk worked as a nutritionist and a professional model. Elon has a younger brother, Kimball and a younger sister, Tosca.

When Elon was eight years old, his parents separated, further exacerbating the harshness of his childhood when South Africa was at that time violent and racism was at its height between the whites and the blacks.

From the very early age, Elon Musk thought about entrepreneurship. He always thought about selling his own video games. He was fond of reading and would stay up in libraries to navigate the world of books.

Elon married his first wife, the Canadian writer, Justin Wilson, while both were students at Queen's University in Ontario. They got married in 2000. Their marriage lasted only eight years, with five children, and then they separated.

In 2008, Elon Musk began dating with an English actress, Talulah Riley, and two years later, married her in January 2012. Four years later,

Elon announced that he had ended his relationship with her. However,

Riley expressed that the marital experience that she had produced a love that would not die forever and that she was sure Elon would make someone happy someday.

Education

The education of Elon Musk was not easy. His schoolmates always made fun of him and beat him. After leaving school, he moved to Canada, where he spent only two years studying at Queen's University. He then moved to Pennsylvania to complete his university studies. He studied physics and economics, got his bachelor's degree and delivered his graduation speech. He was then 26 years old.

The college stage was not easy for Elon as well, as he could not afford to pay for his studies. However, his organization of concerts with his friends enabled him to earn money through a fee imposed on those who attended these events. The number of visitors reached, at times, more than 500, and every one of the attendees would pay $6 for his entry. This income-generating activity helped Elon pay for the cost of his university studies.

The Beginning of Work

Elon Musk's career began at the age of 12. In 1983, he invented the first electronic game and sold it for $500. Elon's passion has helped him pave the way for the establishment of many companies through which he has achieved impressive successes. The following are Elon's career achievements arranged chronologically:

- In 1995, Elon Musk founded, with his brother Campbell, Zip2 Company, and was able to sell it for $ 341 million to Compaq Computer in 1999.
- Later in 1999, Elon founded X.Com, an online banking company

with a capital of $ 10 million.

- In 2000, X-Com merged with Confinity Company, and later became

  PayPal, which specializes on online banking. Elon Musk was the chief executive officer of this leading company in the field of internet banking and electronic payment system.

- In 2002, Elon Musk headed to rocket science, where he invested up to $ 100 million in the establishment of SpaceX, a manufacturer of spacecraft, which provides services related to space transportation.
- In 2003, he founded Tesla Company for electric cars.
- In 2006, he founded Solar City for solar energy services.
- In 2013, he founded Hyperloop, and it is a concept of the high-speed transmission system.
- In 2015, Elon Musk announced the establishment of Open AI Company, a non-profit company specializing in artificial intelligence research, aimed at developing general artificial intelligence in a safe way that benefits humankind.
- In 2016, Elon participated in founding Norlink, a nascent tech company that integrates the human brain with artificial intelligence.
- In 2018, Elon Musk resigns from the Board of Directors of Open AI, to avoid potential future conflict, as he describes it.

Social Life

Elon Musk used to wake up at seven o'clock every morning after only six hours of sleep a day. One of Elon's most important morning rituals is swimming, where he finds rest and relaxation and plenty of space to release his energy during the day.

As for his daily schedule, Elon Musk divides his appointments every five minutes throughout the day, as he is very precise and orderly. He saw that as greater productivity and a higher ability to create achievements.

Elon Musk's working hours is estimated at 85 hours per week, and there are not even two similar days he spends in his life. He spends Monday and Wednesday at *SpaceX* in Los Angeles, and on Tuesdays and

Thursdays, he visits *Tesla*. Elon Musk gives the half-day to a non-profit company in artificial intelligence.

At the end of the week, Elon is committed either to traveling or to spending it with his family consisted of five children. On Saturdays, he sometimes goes to his company, *SpaceX*. "I can be with my children, and at the same time I'm on the e-mail," he says. "If I'm not on mail, I cannot finish my job."

Nevertheless, Elon Musk is keen to keep his work all weekdays; he avoids most of the phone calls, and he has a private and confidential e-mail so that he cannot be disturbed by the messages he does not want to receive from people.

Staff

Elon Musk hires people who see greatness in themselves. One of his most important pieces of advice to every entrepreneur who starts up a project is to attract great characters.

Elon believes that the product or service offered by any employer to customers must be exceptional and distinctive. The employer must discover the best in his staff, and invest in them for the benefit of his project or his company.

Elon Musk has always advises those who work with him to read and take risk. He always tells them, "If you think this work is important, you should try it." He does not ask them to work more or better, but he just invites them to love their work.

At work, Elon always asked for a detailed report on how the project would be completed. He wants accomplishments day by day, hour by hour, and sometimes minute by minute, not week by week or month by month.

"If you are competing with a product that is in the market from the beginning, you have to provide a product or service that is better than the existing one, because you have to put yourself in place of consumers and ask yourself why I should buy this product, not that one which is

reliable, unless there is a big difference, and the more your customers love you, the faster your success is," says Elon Musk.

Painful Past

Elon Musk's family and professional life are not immune to issues and controversies. In 2007, *Tesla* was on the verge of collapse. A year later, the world financial crisis broke out, and *Tesla* continued to lose. In the same year, he separated from his wife after an eight-year marriage that resulted in five children. As a result, he has been exposed to pressures from the press and the media. In 2008, the worst year of his life, Elon Musk woke up on a Sunday, and told himself that he never thought about himself that he could stand neurogenic shocks. *SpaceX* also failed to send a rocket into space after its engine had ignited, that is why he thought about a fourth attempt, in which he succeeded, proving to everyone who told him, "You will not be able to succeed." Elon Musk considered 2008 the worst year of his life, but he remembers that year with his experiences and the solutions he has created.

Challenges

Elon Musk fought to effect some changes to his system of work. He preferred Microsoft, while Max Levchin favored Linux, which led to the disagreement of his members and partners.

One day when Elon was traveling to Australia on a mission, when he was the CEO of *PayPal* — he received a letter saying he was removed from duty in favor of Thiel. The news was a shock to Elon, but his wife, Justin, invited him to a deal. Elon immediately returned from his journey to start dealing with this decision. When he had arrived at the company's headquarters, he got into a heated discussion with the members about that decision, but when it became clear to him what the decision was, and that the company took that decision to move forward in a way that is in favor of work, he surrendered to reality and said, "In

fact, I did not want to become the CEO of that company, but I think there are some important things that should happen, and if I'm not the CEO, I'm not sure it will happen, but when I talked to Max and Peter, it became clear to me they're going to do these matters, and they will make it happen. I knew that it is not the end of the world, especially since I own the largest stake in *PayPal*."

Work was more important to Elon Musk than anything else. He even said, "I wish there was a way that enabled me to do without eating, in return for more work. I wish there was a way through which I could get the nutrients without sitting down to eat a meal." Elon thought, spending time eating was a big challenge for him and it is a waste of his time.

Elon Musk was afraid that Russia would assassinate him after he managed to develop *SpaceX*, which managed to compete with the world's most powerful companies at a lower cost. "When you try many things, you learn more from failure than you learn from success," he says.

Passion

Elon Musk believes that success in work is the ability to work on more than one task; work for as many hours as possible; and work to bring out the best of what lies within those who work with him, of skills and talents.

Always love what you do and do what you love. Elon always says to those who work with him, and always advises them to find what motivates them and calls them to wake up early every morning.

Elon Musk's creations did not stop. He invented the Hyperloop, a high-speed train that travels through an empty tube, moving people from one state to another, in a short time. It shortens the distance between Los Angeles and San Francisco to 30 minutes, surpassing congestion with many times the speed of other transportation. All this creativity comes despite his preoccupation with his other companies;

SpaceX and *Tesla*.

Dream and Goal

Elon Musk always thinks that goals are possible. Although he sees impossible targets as frustrating, he does not want people to hit their head on the wall. He does not set impossible goals, but he is always optimistic; he is a realistic man.

Elon Musk writes in his memoirs that he can retire and buy a private island somewhere and live in it, but this is not his ultimate goal.

The Turning Point

When Elon Musk decided to begin his actual steps to complete the project through which he aspires to conquer the outer space, he communicated with Russia to buy missiles, but they told him that the value of the missile was $ 8 million, which led him to building his own missile at a lower cost.

In 2002, Elon founded *SpaceX* from the money he acquired through his sale of *PayPal*. *SpaceX* is an American company specializing in space technology industries, as well as space flights.

At the beginning of the establishment of *SpaceX*, the company had few employees and had an empty office in Los Angeles. Today, the company is one of the largest space technology companies with more than 5,000 people.

The goal of Elon Musk is to create a spacecraft at a lower cost than normal, and to help send the first person to Mars. He created a spacecraft called *Dragon*, which was a great achievement after everyone had challenged him and declared it has been difficult for him to achieve. However, *SpaceX* failed to send the missile on its first three attempts. Elon Musk, however, said in his opening statement, after the last attempt failed, that they were going to try again within a month. On the fourth attempt, he succeeded to prove all those questioning his ability

wrong.

Elon Musk made the first successful launch of *SpaceX* on September 28, 2008, where it took four attempts to achieve the goal that seemed impossible to others. Through that experience, Elon advises everyone, who wants to achieve his goal, to never surrender, but to take a step toward risk to achieve his goal, and never fear failure. A successful person is one who corrects his mistakes and learns from them, but failure is one who denies his mistakes.

Persistence and Continuity

Elon Musk was once asked about his failure for the third time in a row, whether he would give up or not, but he answered that he would not give up at all. Shortly after that, he received a call from *NASA*, where the two parties agreed to conclude a contract, which is worth $ 1.5 billion, to deliver supplies for outer space. Elon asked them if they intended to reach Mars a day. They answered that they had not a plan at that time to achieve that. He told them that he wanted human civilization to leave the earth to Mars and that he would be delighted that people would take steps toward the colonization of Mars.

Elon Musk's insistence on achieving his goal was represented in perseverance and non-withdrawal. He said that he had nothing to regret. He spent days traveling from one state to another, and this was almost daily, to run his companies.

Elon is famous for reading anything that falls into his hands from the moment he wakes up in the morning, until he sleeps at night. This simply indicates his constant love of learning.

Success

Elon Musk has achieved successive achievements, as a result of his passion and determination. His most notable achievements are as follows:

- In 2003, he founded Tesla for electric motors, which aims to create a sustainable energy shift in the future.
- In 2008, Tesla manufactured the Roadster.
- In 2013, Tesla was awarded the Best Car of the Year Award.
- In 2015, Tesla received the highest safety assessment of the year, and in the same year, it produced the Powerwall, a low-cost solar home charger that can be used during power outages.
- In 2017, Tesla manufactured Model three Cars.

The genius of Elon Musk created a revolution in transportation, both on land and in space, as SpaceX's valued for more than $20 billion, according to a report by Forbes site.

Funding

In 1995, Elon and his brother Campbell founded *Zip2*, with the participation of a number of investors He was able to sell it to *Compaq Computer* at $341 million in 1999. This led to Elon Musk's increase in shares worth $22 million, which he then invested $10 million to establish *X.com*. In 2002, when *PayPal* was sold to *eBay*, Elon Musk earned $165 million as profits. In the same year, 2002, Elon invested $100 million, taken from the amount he had received, to set up *SpaceX*.

Elon Musk is the CEO of *SpaceX* and *Tesla*, and he is known as the Iron Man. The character of the film of Iron Man was based on him. He was the inspiration for creating the character which some of its film scenes were filmed in *SpaceX*.

Elon Musk and his *SpaceX* entered history when the company launched a rocket into space, a spacecraft called *Falcon 9*, that transported supplies to astronauts aboard the International Space Station; becoming the first private company to send a spacecraft to the International Space Station. Elon commented on this event, "I feel fortunate. We feel like we have won a huge prize."

He says, "I am happy with what I have achieved. I always seek to make the world a better place. Everyone has to like what he does. If otherwise, he has to realize that life is short. When he likes what he does, then he will think about it, even when he does not do it. If he does not like what he does, then he will not succeed."

Giving

When Elon Musk began showing great interest in artificial intelligence, he launched *Open AI*, with capital amounting to nearly $ 1 billion. It is a non-profit organization, specializing in artificial intelligence research. Open AI aims to promote and develop artificial intelligence systems to serve humanity. All company staff and researchers are eager to achieve that goal.

Lifestyle now

Elon Musk has been able to make a fortune after a series of challenges. He has turned them into successes that serve his ambition for wealth and influence all over the world. In 2018, his fortune reached $20 billion, according to a report by Forbes site.

As for his health, Elon works out in a sports club once or twice a week. He is keen on healthful food, even though he drinks diet Cola.

Mark Cuban
"The Fierce shark."

6

Mark Cuban, the Fierce shark

Childhood and Family

Mark Cuban was born in Pennsylvania in 1958, and comes from a middle-income family consisted of five, his parents and three siblings of whom he is the eldest. His father worked in car upholstery, and always advised Mark that if he wanted something, he would have to achieve it. He never told him he could not, but encouraged him to have experience, for there was nothing to lose.

Mark discovered his love of commerce at a young age. At 10, he sold baseball cards, repackaged the cards with special cards and sold them at a bigger price. Two years later, he moved on to selling garbage bags to houses. After three years, at fifteen years old, he began buying and selling stamps.

Education

Mark Cuban wanted to take business lessons at the age of 16, but his secondary school did not offer classes in this field. He joined the University of Indiana for business and because it was the least expensive university around.

Mark liked challenges very much. In his first year at the university, he studied the final year subjects because he wanted to begin with hard materials to save the easy subjects for his last year. He wanted the final year in college to be easy and a comfortable year. In 1980, Mark completed his undergraduate studies at the University of Indiana.

The Beginning of Work

Mark Cuban began his career immediately after graduating from college. He started working at Mellon Bank in Pittsburgh for nine months. After that, he moved to Tronex 2000 in Andean, USA. It was a company specializing in repairing TVs. Mark's job was to sell the company's brand to repairing stores by making phone calls. This did not last for more than nine months. Then, he moved from one place to another for work, but did not continue in any of them for a long time due to several reasons, most notably he discovered that some of the work he was doing did not fit his vision of the future. He convinced himself that every action he was doing paid him to learn, and that experience would be valuable if he knew what he wanted to be.

After his experiences in Pittsburgh, Mark moved to Dallas, to work in *Your Business Software Store* that specializes in computer programs.

Mark spent most of his spare time reading guidebooks, giving him enough information to provide advice to and gain customer confidence. During his term in office, he advised companies and installed software for an additional fee. Nine months later, Mark was dismissed.

Social Life

Mark spends more than three hours a day reading. He spent days off, reading computer files, books and magazines. "The reasons that led me to be a distinctive employee or a businessman were reading books and magazines," he says. It is true that this information is available to all and cheap, but most people do not want the information that gives them precedence in their field.

One of Mark's habits is working once he wakes up every morning. The first thing he does is look at the messages he receives on e-mail. When he gets an idea into his mind, he immediately wakes up in the middle of the night to work on them, and sometimes he wakes up several times to write down those ideas.

Mark Cuban was celebrating much and was fun with his teammates, especially after having achieved something. He has been celebrating almost daily since moving to Dallas.

When he was asked about his friends who spent his time with them, Mark says that "It is easy to find your friend, whom you see as truthful, among those who befriend you for money. I still befriend my classmates and friends when I moved to Dallas, but I am not looking for new friends."

Staff

He started his first project after being fired in the same field he worked in, which was selling and installing computer software, and consulting in the field. He founded *Microsoft*. However, he did not own an office, store, computer, or even the computer software he sold. He used the home phone to contact his customers who had previously worked with them to offer his services. Mark Cuban collaborated with Martin Woodall, an owner of a company working in the field of computer software. Mark provided computer stuff, and Martin provided accounting programs. The nice thing about this cooperation was that Martin offered Mark to work in an office.

"If you're working in any area close to technology, you have to work as if your competitors are big companies like *Google, Microsoft, and Facebook*, even if they are not in your field because you do not know when they will enter this field. Always be prepared to face top companies."

One of Mark Cuban's top tips for entrepreneurs is to make the work fun for employees, not to make offices closed. Open offices give staff power. It is important that the employer monitors the level of achievement of his employees and rewards them for their work and achievement. It is also important for an entrepreneur to choose the partner who has what he lacks. Mark used to describe meetings as wasting time unless they were to make a deal. Many ways of communications shorten the meeting and give better results.

Painful Past

When Mark Cuban moved to Dallas, he had nothing but his *1977 Model Fiat*. He slept on the floor, his wardrobe was a pile of clothes lying on the ground, and he shared a three-bedroom apartment with five persons. He did not have a job to make money at that time, as he was living off restaurant offerings and free food served in bars.

Mark has learned a valuable lesson in his second year of founding *Microsoft*. His secretary stole $ 83,000 from the company account by switching names in the checks that were supposed to be for suppliers. He did not have the money to sue her; therefore, he took out his rage through hard work, for the secretary to return the money she had stolen. Then, he closely watched his staff, trusted in them, and then worked with them on the principle of mutual respect.

Challenges

Mark Cuban always repeats this saying, "It does not matter how many times you fail, no matter how many times you were close to success, as no one will care about your failure, and you are not supposed to care about them as well. It is important to succeed once, and people, no matter how difficult or unsuccessful conditions you have encountered, will see your success as a stroke of luck that has been achieved overnight.

Anyone who encounters moments of frustration, fatigue, and failure, and the successful person is the person who fights those feelings to get out of them strongly, smartly and fast.

When Mark Cuban was offered to invest in *Uber Company*, he refused to participate, because it conflicted with many taxi regulations, and he saw that might create some problems. But he learned from this experience that if a person believes in something then, he should not look at laws and regulations first, but must start with the implementation, and look at regulatory matters later.

Passion

Mark Cuban believes that anyone will manage to know his passion through experience, but he has to discover it. Mark was aware of his passion for commerce when he was young, but he did not discover his passion for technology until he worked in the bank, where they worked on the electronic system. One does not know his passion until he tries. He loved working on computers so much that he used to forget himself, and did not know how much time he had spent on; he thought it was still six or seven pm, while it was one o'clock or two in the morning. He even used to forget to eat when working.

"Everyone has one or two things that are inherently ingenious," says Mark Cuban. "The hard thing is to find it and have the confidence to go that way. One has to learn about his skills, to look for a place where he can use these skills and then set out. If his choices are correct, he will undoubtedly make a fortune."

Dream and goal

Mark Cuban was fond of basketball, but he did not have the skill to be a player but became the owner of his favorite team. When he moved to Dallas, he set up a list of the fields he wanted to work with. He always said that one should not follow the things that inspire them. Rather, he must follow the things on which he makes his effort and his time, as well as masters his work because the man loves to be good at something.

When you see people who have ideas and turn them into distinct

companies, that conveys a message that everyone with an idea they are trying to achieve can make it a reality on the ground, and it can be something special.

Turning Point

A customer asked Mark Cuban for the installation of the software for his company. The time that was best for him was at 9am, but the opening of the store was at 9:30am. He asked the permission of his manager, and he was refused. However, Mark saw it as a good deal where he was supposed to receive a commission of $1500. He made the decision to ask his lady colleague to come to open the store earlier, for him to be able to install the software on the computers of the company. The next day, Mark returned to work with a check for $15,000, and his manager dismissed him for not following the orders.

Mark felt frustrated, and thought of himself as a failure, but he had bills to pay. He decided to start his own business instead of getting into the cycle of job-search again.

Persistence and Continuity

Marc Cuban measures effort by not counting the hours he spent working. The effort is measured by how one achieves, and what the outcome is. Business success is either one's commitment to achieving results or not.

Success

Success does not come neither through your money nor through your acquaintances. Instead, it comes with the will and courage to succeed. Mark Cuban recommended that for everyone around him. He says that entrepreneurship is competition 24 hours a day, seven days a week, and 365 days a year. A person must exert effort to work, to learn and to

make success a priority in his life.

Mark Cuban sees that everyone can succeed. Everyone has the idea of success. Everybody dreams of success. However, what makes successful people is the ability to working on that dream. All you need is to succeed once, then successes will be easy to achieve. Mark points out that time is more important than money, and it is not important that any employer see the cup half full or half empty, but it is important he should be the one who pours the water out of that cup, so he has to be the ruler of his life. He should take every opportunity that allows him to be the controller. Mark does not believe that there is a formula for success, but he believes that a person can prepare himself for success. One has to be smart and has to exert more effort than his rivals do.

When Mark Cuban was asked how he treats himself as a famous person, he said, "Why should I be someone other than what I am? I love my way of life. I want to do what I want. So, why should I change?" He means by this is that his fame and wealth did not change his lifestyle.

Mark says there is no downside in being a wealthy person. Being rich, Mark Cuban did not keep a low profile. Rather, he was sitting with masses in games and celebrations. As a famous character, Marc Cuban receives requests or project ideas every moment. He hears others for 30 seconds to decide whether he wants to hear them from the beginning or not.

Funding

Mark Cuban saw debt as the biggest obstacle to human destiny, whether it is personal debt or project finance. The more people committed to paying, the harder it is for a person to focus on himself and to discover what happens.

Mark likens the one who takes money from an investor to that who plays by investor's rules, as the investor is not interested in the dreams of that who takes his money to invest. Rather, he is interested in money. When a person deviates from the promise he made to the investor, then his dreams will go off a cliff.

According to Mark Cuban, there are two sources of money for any entrepreneur to start his business; either the money is from the entrepreneur's pocket, or it is from the pocket of customers. Mark advises everyone around him not to borrow money from anyone, even if they are members of their family, as the family is not like investors who do not care about their dreams, and you do not want to feel guilty if you lose the money you have raised for investment.

Giving

In 2003, Mark created *Fallen Patriot Foundation*, which is a charitable project for the families of soldiers killed and wounded in the Iraq war. He donated $1 million from the shares of *Mark Cuban Foundation*, a charitable organization run by his brother, Bryan. Mark Cuban is known for donation to charitable organizations within and outside the city of Dallas.

In 2014, Mark ensured the marriage of a couple with cancer who did not have the money to have a wedding. He says he does these charitable deeds because he pleases himself, but he does not like what he does to be covered by the media, because he does not do this to make a show of his deeds.

Lifestyle now

Mark Cuban believes that a person should undergo a comprehensive medical examination of himself every three months as a preventive health check. "The difference between being a millionaire and being a billionaire is like the difference between having a cent and having a thousand dollars," Mark says regarding wealth. "There are many things you can do or buy." In 1990, Mark Cuban sold his computer company for $ 6 million. Immediately afterward, he traded in shares with $ 2 million and was able to turn it into a $ 20 million profit,

enabling him to establish, with his partner Todd Wagner, an online gaming company called *AudioNet* in 1995. Three years after the company's great success, he renamed it as *Broadcast.com*. By 2000, Mark and Todd decided to sell the company to *Yahoo Group*, with a value of $ 5.7 billion.

By 2018, Mark Cuban has a fortune of about $ 3.7 billion, and he is investing in more than 134 companies, including *Dallas Mavericks* basketball team, and *XTV* channel and *DropBox*.

Larry Page
"The Knight of search engines."

7

Larry Page, the Knight of Search Engines

Childhood and Family

L awrence Edward Page was born in Michigan in 1973. He grew up in a highly educated family. His father, Karl Page, a Ph.D. in computer science, was one of the most famous lecturers in his field at the University of Michigan. His mother, Gloria Page, had a master's degree in computer science and was a database consultant. The family's interest in computers has been reflected in Larry's life since he was young, and when his family acquired its first computer when Larry was five years old.

Larry inherited the habit of controversy from his father. He and his father always engaged in discussions and controversies about any subject. His parents separated when he was eight years old, but he did not feel that he had lost one of them, as his father visited him constantly.

Education

Larry Page studied at Montessori Primary School.

Larry graduated from the University of Michigan with a degree in computer engineering, and obtained an A grade with honors. Then,

he went to California to complete his doctoral studies at Stanford University, where he met his future partner Sergey Brin, who was in the second year, and who was leading the university instructing tour for new students.

As soon as Larry Page had joined Stanford University, he began working on his science project, a search engine that analyzed the links between websites and arranged search results by analysis. He called it *backRup* and worked on it with his colleague Sergei. He chose Stanford University to complete his studies because he was thinking of two options; the first was to get Ph.D. and work as a professor, and the other option was to start his own project in the field of computers. Stanford University was the choice because it was a strong university in the field of computer science and close to Silicon Valley, where the largest technology companies are located. The University also provides great facilities for inventors and developers to transform their ideas into projects.

The Beginning of Work

Larry Page offered a proposal to change the name of their innovation, and the name *Google* was chosen, which means number one followed by 100 zero regarding the information provided by this site. The growth of *Google* at Stanford University was remarkable and influential. It was the first site of searches of students, lecturers and researchers.

Larry and Sergey decided to offer their project for sale because they did not have the financial capacity to expand the servers, and their entry into the world of entrepreneurship means they would leave their studies, which they did not want to do. They presented their idea to the greatest research companies at that time such as *Yahoo*, and *America Online*, which used employees to analyze and categorize sites, but they rejected the offer on the grounds that the current method meets the purpose and that search engines do not bring financial returns. Larry and Sergey stuck to their ideas and dreams of spreading information

to as many people as possible and decided to leave their studies to establish *Google* despite the strong objections from their families.

Social Life

The environment, in which Larry Page has lived since childhood, was an academic environment, which focused on studies and learning. One of Larry's most important friends is Sergey Brin, his university fellow and co-founder of *Google*. Sergey has many things in common with Larry: highly educated family, studied at the Montessori system of education, love mathematics, and aspired to earn a Ph.D.

One of Larry's friends is also Elon Musk, and they often spent time together. When Larry was asked whether he would donate money after his death, he responded that he preferred to give his fortune to thinkers such as Elon Musk rather than to charities; as that would be more beneficial to humanity. One of his fellows is Richard Branson who was chosen by Larry to be his best man at his wedding.

Staff

The search engine's eternal problem is how to get money from this process. Other companies' thinking goes to advertising, but Larry Page saw its presence in the search engines as very annoying for those logging into the internet, but it is the only way to gain from search engines. Therefore, he thought about a new way to show ads so that they are not annoying. He produced *Google Ad*, a way of advertising by showing the ad that matches a person's search, and the total amount of the ad is calculated by the number of people who clicked on the ad link through the search engine. This process was convenient for the advertised companies and for those logging into the internet as well.

Larry has been very interested in the work environment since *Google* was founded, creating a fun family environment that calls for creativity and development. Among Larry's core rules of management and that

which he encouraged his employees to do are the following:

Do not delay business at all, and conduct matters as soon as possible.

Do not interfere in anyone's way. If one does not have a value to add, then he should let others accomplish this work.

Do not be bureaucratic.

Ideas are more important than age, so young people deserve respect and cooperation.

The worst thing one can do is to stop someone else from working without discussing with him and finding a better way to accomplish the task.

Painful Past

In 2001, *Kleiner Perkins Caufield & Belize* and *Sequoia Capital* invested $ 50 million in *Google*, which put pressure on Larry Page to step down as CEO of *Google* on the grounds that the company needed to have a mature administration that is characterized by experience. Larry accepted the idea and stepped down after he had sought the advice of Steve Jobs, the CEO of *Apple* and Eric Schmidt, who became the CEO of the company after leaving his post as CEO of *Novell*. At this time, both the staff and the new CEO saw that Larry was still the leader, and his influence was evident in making decisions. Among those decisions was the purchase of *Android*, which was not clear to Erik until the last time. Larry returned to his position as CEO of *Google* in 2011, and he felt that this period had helped him remarkably for innovation and development.

Challenges

One of the problems that Larry Page faced during his development of *Google site*, his university project, was the search and classification process was a major burden. Larry thought about inventing a method that no one had ever used, which was connecting PCs to one

another. This method created fast search and high storage space. The idea was beneficial. When *Google* had later rented a warehouse to save its servers, it disposed of unnecessary pieces, reducing the space required for each server, and costs.

Passion

One of the most important skills that Larry Page gained in early life was creative thinking. Montessori's teaching style has helped develop his creativity and leadership skills. When he was at the University of Michigan, he rolled in a range of leadership programs. He also served as president of the Institute of Electrical and Electronics Engineers, *Eta Kappa Nu*. This helped him a lot when he started the foundation of *Google*. Larry was talented in mathematics and analysis, and his passion for computers since childhood was a key motivation for choosing his specialization and working to integrate all of these together until *Google*'s success became predictable.

Dream and Goal

Larry Page's goal was to obtain a Ph.D., but once, he woke up in the middle of the night because of a strange dream. In the dream, he could download the entire world's web pages on his computer. This dream has created the way that made Google the fastest search engine in the world. This dream was the reason for *Google*'s foundation. This is what brought back the dream of his boyhood, which is the invention of something that makes the world a better place. Since his invention of Google, Larry has focused on facilitating the search and delivery of information to the largest number of people around the world. This is what Google has been able to do today. "One has to put dreams that make him enthusiastic for his work for 10 years. In this way, even if one did not achieve his dream, he will find something in his way that will make him more passionate and enthusiastic," says Larry.

Turning Point

One of the most important turning points in Larry Page's life was when he read the biography of Nikolai Tesla at 12 years old. He was deeply influenced by him and took him as an example. He converted his message into working on inventing something that makes the world better. This has made him dispose of his dream to pursue a Ph.D., and be a lecturer like his father. Larry is still looking for ways to make the world better. He has invested in many fields, such as natural energy, space science, robotics.

Persistence and Continuity

Larry Page calls on people to accept change and development. This principle has been implanted in *Google* since its foundation. He also warns of one's stagnation and complacency, calling for the continuity and improvement of self-development. One of Larry's pieces of advice to entrepreneurs is to focus on long-term goals and what really concerns them. Larry has a method called the toothbrush test; if one uses a thing more than his use of toothbrush a day, then this thing is essential for him. If the number of these things increases, then he should put them in a list and arrange them according to importance, so that anyone can spend his time in favor of the things that concern him first.

Success

Success in Larry Page's perspective is the ability to solve a big number of problems. "When you try to solve a big problem, it may be easier than solving the small problem. A big problem is that which many people suffer from, and when you intend to solve it, it motivates people to help you solve it, making it easier to solve. If you want success, you should not be afraid of failure. The person, who wants to succeed, has to fail

much and in the shortest possible time to achieve success quickly," says Larry in this context.

Google has been expanding globally since its foundation, and Larry has sought to facilitate this spread. He thought of launching Google translator that would make it easier for its users to search in any other languages. Trying to find Google translator was not easy, but Larry and the team accepted the challenge. Twelve years after its launch, Google translator could translate into 103 languages.

Funding

The foundation of *Google* needed big capital. David Sheraton, one of Larry Page's professors at the university, suggested meeting one of his friends, Andy Bechtolsheim, the Vice President of *Cisco*, and a proponent of new ideas. When Larry presented the idea to Andy, he liked it so much, describing it as the best idea he has heard since years. He gave him a check for $ 100,000 to support his company without negotiation, discussion or knowing that *Google* has not yet been established. The check remained for two weeks until a bank account was officially opened and registered. This led to a sense of confidence, which led Larry to offer investments in the company to friends and family. As a result, he was able to raise a fortune, which was worth one million dollars, to establish the company.

Giving

In 2006, Larry Page created a charity called *Carl Page Charitable Foundation*, which refers to his father and in recognition of him. It is a charity dedicated to education and health, helping the poor and solving family problems. Larry manages this incorporation himself and has donated several times with shares from *Google*. He has donated to this incorporation several times, including in 2014, as he donated shares, which are worth up to 177 million dollars.

Lifestyle now

In 2007, Larry Page married Lucinda Southworth and rented a private island for a week for the wedding, which cost between $ 2 million and $ 3 million.

By 2018, Larry's fortune is $ 48.8 billion, and he is the CEO of his *Alphabet Inc.*, which includes *Google Group* valued at 766.4 billion dollars.

Oprah Winfrey
"The Humanity Ambassador"

8

Oprah Winfrey, The Humanity Ambassador

Childhood and Family

Oprah Winfrey was born in 1954 in the US State of Mississippi, a state that widely witnessed racism at that time. During that period, it was common for a white man to accuse or ridicule a black-skinned man in the street.

She lived with her parents Vernon Winfrey and Vernita Lee, together with her grandparents, in challenging circumstances. The family was so poor that at six years old, Oprah wore clothes made from potato bags.

Oprah says she grew up in a rural environment, where people raised fruits and vegetables and some animals. She helped her grandmother pick fruits from the garden next to their house.

In her childhood, Oprah Winfrey often felt lonely, but she knew that her survival depended on caring for herself.

In her youth, Oprah loved to have her friends at her grandmother's house. After her friends had left, she would feel scared staying alone with her grandmother, who had dementia, as she described her. Oprah had books and dolls made at home. She would perform household chores and talked to animals with specific names.

Education

At kindergarten, Oprah's teacher saw that she had a very high level of intelligence, which prompted her to ask the principal to take her to the first grade. She was superior in all stages of her studies. In 1969, she earned the title Most Popular Student in East Nashville high school because of her distinguished relationship with teachers and students.

For a long time, Oprah wanted to be a successful person. "Be distinguished!" was the best advice she had for everyone around her. She considered excellence the real tool for success. She said, "If one wants the world to give him the best he wants, then he should give the world the best he has."

Oprah Winfrey was able to outperform her fellow students in all levels until she became one of the first American students of African origin. She received an education grant to enroll at the University of Tennessee, where she graduated with a Bachelor of Arts degree in Theater Arts.

The Beginning of Work

At 19, Oprah Winfrey worked in Nashville TV. She was the youngest broadcaster on a television channel. In 1982, she was involved in a local news radio, which made *WSS* executives admire her. They had already asked her to go to their headquarters in Chicago to try out a cooking program there. Although she did not know anything about cooking, it did not stop her from trying and experimenting. It was natural for her to be afraid of accepting a job that she was unfamiliar with, but she overcame this by her constant ability to confront fears.

After her experience with *WBS*, she moved to *ABC International* where she offered them to adopt her own cooking program but was rejected. She felt very resentful at that time, but she did not let that hinder the progress of her life. She did not allow anything to diminish her dreams.

87

In 1985, Oprah Winfrey began acting, playing a leading role in Steven Spielberg's film " *The Color Purple*," which was nominated for nine

Oscar awards. Therefore, TV and movie offers came to her because of her great success.

In 1989, she was able to create her own program, "*Oprah Show*," which had achieved global success. It was a daily program that tackled social issues of interest to the American community. The exceptional success of the program could be attributed to her excellent presentation and the engaging conversation with her guest. She has become a prominent media model worldwide.

Social Life

In 1976, Oprah Winfrey interviewed Gayle King, a news presenter of a television station in Baltimore, while Oprah was the assistant production manager in the same TV station. Both Oprah and Gayle did not become friends immediately. They were only two women who respected and supported each other's career, but soon they laughed together as very good friends. Oprah recalls the depth of her friendship with Gayle. She says, "Gayle helped me in my times of failure, and she shared everything with me to a great extent. She has never judged me. Gayle has been the most encouraging of me in all my successes."

In her childhood, Oprah Winfrey did not have many friends. She rarely went out for entertainment. She lived in different apartments, but did not give herself time to get to know the neighbors who lived next door or opposite hers.

In 2004, she moved to a beautiful house in California. At this point, Oprah recalls that a new world had been opened for her. After spending many years under the spotlight, she had become sociable for the first time in her life. Now, she found herself looking forward to going out, laughing and communicating with others.

For Oprah Winfrey, books were a way of escapism and an opportunity to be anywhere she chose. She believed that reading showed her the reality, and allowed her to reach anything that her mind could absorb.

Ever since she was a child, Oprah has loved growing vegetables in her grandfather's garden. In her grandfather's house, she used to make blueberry scones with lemon every morning. For reading books, it was a daily habit for Oprah, whatever the weather and conditions were. The oak tree next to their house was her favorite spot to sit in for long hours reading.

Staff

In 1988, when Oprah Winfrey introduced *Oprah Show* for the first time on television, she had to buy a studio and hire all the producers. There were many things that Oprah did not realize at that time. She made many mistakes during the first years of her career, but fortunately, she was not very famous at that time, as she was able to learn the lessons and went through it getting better at a steady pace.

In 1999, Oprah managed to purchase her show. In the same year, she founded *Oxygen Media*, a company dedicated to producing cable and internet programming for women.

Painful Past

When Oprah Winfrey was 12 years old, she lived with her mother after living with her grandparents. For years, Oprah hid a secret that nobody knew until she felt safe enough to share with others. Between 10 and 14 years old, she was subjected to numerous attacks, which got her involved in many relationships. She became pregnant at 14 years old. She felt ashamed and dishonored. She hid her pregnancy until her doctor noticed her swollen ankle and belly. She gave birth in 1968, but her baby died in the hospital several weeks later. Then, Oprah Winfrey returned to complete her education at school, and did not tell anyone about her pregnancy and the dead baby.

However, this incident did not go unnoticed in Oprah's life. It had a direct impact in her life. She became addicted to narcotic and hallucinogenic pills during her adolescence, and advanced to heroin

and cocaine abuse.

At that stage, Oprah's mother, who lost control of her, wanted to send her to Juvenile Hall rehabilitation center. Unfortunately, Oprah did not have a place there, so her mother decided to send her to live with her father, a businessperson in Nashville. Her father disciplined her with iron grip. Oprah's life changed, and she began realizing her responsibilities.

Challenges

At 15 years old, Oprah Winfrey earned 50 cents an hour, for babysitting Mrs. Abshari's two sons, whom she described as very ornery.

She later worked briefly in a cheap goods store for $1.5 an hour. Her job was to fold socks and organize the merchandize in the shelves neatly.

Oprah was not allowed to be responsible for the cash register or even to talk to customers, the reason she quickly disliked her job at the store. She realized it was impossible to live like this and earn money that way. She left her job and went to work in her father's store, but she was not paid for her work. However, what Oprah wanted was to talk to people even without being paid.

By the time she was 17, Oprah Winfrey had worked in radio for $100 a week.

When she reached the age of 19, Oprah moved to work in *Nashville TV*. She says, "I suffered from a failure in my first career when I was discussing about the channel news producer so that he could not stand that anymore. Therefore, I was dismissed to read the news because I become sentimental when reading the news as a news reporter in the evening news. Instead, I was offered a role in a day program."

A few years later, Oprah Winfrey was sent to Los Angeles as a young television reporter working in *WGZ TV* in the city of Baltimore to interview some of the television stars. It was a great opportunity for her to prove that she would perform so brilliantly without the usual

help of her fellow announcer, and saw this as an addition to her fame, as well as her professional experience. However, when she arrived in California, she felt as if she were a small fish dumped in the Hollywood Aquarium. She began to doubt her abilities, and she said to herself, "Who am I to think I can actually enter their world and expect them to talk to me?"

The first step for Oprah in Hollywood was to invite all news reporters from all over the country, each of whom had five minutes to talk to one of the actors, after which she began to feel comfortable and reassured that she was brilliant.

Passion

Oprah Winfrey was fond of reporting the stories of others, extracting the truth from their experiences, and converting them into proverbs that could teach, inspire or benefit someone else.

In her childhood, Oprah wished to be a good actor until she thought she would be a religious preacher at some point. On a weekday, she went to the house of worship, sat on the wooden bench, and recorded everything the cleric said in a notebook.

Today, Oprah Winfrey's influence on societies has overtaken the influence of universities, politicians and the clergy. By the end of the 20th century, she has become at the top of the list of the most affluent Americans with African origins and one of the most fabulous women in the history of American society. *Life Magazine* has listed her within the ten characters that have changed the world, and Oprah was the only one of those characters who is still alive.

Dream and Goal

In her life, Oprah Winfrey aimed to have the best possible life. "Somewhere inside myself, even when I was a teenager, I felt that something bigger was hidden for me, but it was not about making a fortune or

fame at all. It was about being a better human being, and it was about challenging myself to achieve excellence at all levels," she says.

Oprah sees that one must not dream of material prosperity directly, because it is about creating a life full of joy and peace of mind. In her life's journey, she has learned that wealth cannot certainly create a sense of peace inside you. The meaning of being a living person is becoming the person you were supposed to be, and having the courage to realize your dream, no matter what anyone else will say or think.

One of Oprah Winfrey's most important tips for those, who seek to achieve their dreams, is to gather all the strength and activity as possible as they can, and then release them. Oprah has always considered the importance of focusing heavily on using time, interests and resources to let a generation of courageous women advance, a generation who can establish themselves and know their strengths.

Turning Point

On one memorable day in 1969, a religious leader named, Jackson, lit up her enthusiasm and changed the way she looked at life. She listened to his speech about the personal sacrifices made by the first ancestors, until they managed to have a stable life in the United States, regardless of how they came.

Jackson was a great advocate of excellence, and he said, "Excellence is the best deterrent to racial discrimination." Oprah took his words seriously at that time, and from then she wrote her favorite proverb,

"If you want to be successful, then you have to be distinct. If you want the world to offer you the best, then offer the world the best you have."

Oprah Winfrey considers that moment, when she decided to put the sign after she was influenced by the words of the cleric, as the spark of excellence and nobility in her stage of education over all of her colleagues, until she received an educational grant through which she achieved a bachelor's degree in theatrical arts.

Persistence and Continuity

When it comes to emotional and social issues and speaking to a wide audience, Oprah Winfrey sees that as the right environment for success. She says, "This environment makes something happen between her and those she shares talk and discussion with." She adds, "I can feel what they feel and I can feel that they are responding to me immediately because I know with certainty of mind than anything, I have experienced or felt with anyone I talk to, arises from being aware that we are all on the same path. We all want the same things: love, joy and appreciation."

"Insistence is steadfastness," says Oprah Winfrey. "Strength is our ability to resist and overcome resistance. This does not mean that people, who persevere, do not feel afraid and tired, as they have such feelings, but the most difficult moments are those through which we can trust that if we take just one step more than we feel capable of it, and if we take advantage of the wonderful insistence that everyone has — then we will learn some of the most profound lessons; those lessons that life necessarily gives us.

Oprah sees one will encounter challenges wherever one's journey is. Stability in the face of challenges is a great blessing. It enables you to be able to continue your journey.

Oprah advises everyone persevering in his life that when he is able to see the obstacles as they are, then he should not lose his self-confidence at all costs. Therefore, if everyone, who has taken his course toward achieving his goal, knows that his mistakes and failures are a starting point for the future, then this is a clear sign that he is moving in the right direction.

Success

After her impressive success, Oprah Winfrey opened her own radio station, named *Oprah and Friends*, and also launched *Oprah Magazine*, as well as she began her own channel, *OWN*, which is broadcast free of charge in more than 70 million homes. In addition to her establishment of *Harpo studios*, which are subject to her company.

Her first film appearance was in 1985 in *Steven Spielberg film*, and she won nominations from the Academy and the Golden Globes for her role in the movie.

She then established her own production company called *Harpo*, the reverse of the word *Oprah*, and established her own studio in Chicago to become the third woman with a production company. By 1997, she had made a fortune, which was worth $ 96 million.

She wrote five books, including her book on weight loss, which she published with her trainer in 2005, and made enormous profits around the world, and it was on the list of bestsellers until the book of *Memoirs of President Bill Clinton* came to beat it.

In the early 1990s, all of Oprah Winfrey's talk shows turned out to be, according to her, trivial, except for *Oprah Show*, as this show became more popular with time, becoming an integral part of American popular culture, where it was a platform related to all the details of their lives. For Oprah Winfrey to film several historical episodes with the stars and symbols of American society, she had to set a goal to reach more than 100 countries around the world.

Oprah Show has attracted millions of viewers from all over the world and has achieved great wealth and has become the longest in the history of television.

Oprah Winfrey was known as a literary critic and a leading news anchor, making her the second most influential character in the world according to *Forbes Magazine* in 2005, as well as one of the wealthiest persons. The last episode of her program was on 25 May 2011, after she decided to retire permanently, and devote her time to managing her own satellite channel *OWN*.

The Hollywood Association of Foreign Press has granted her the *Golden Globe Cecil B. DeMille Award*, which is annually granted to an influential character in the world of arts and entertainment, at the seventy-fourth

Golden Globe Awards Ceremony. After that win, *CNN* published a report which has created a furor about Oprah Winfrey's intention to run for the US presidential elections in 2020.

After a spectacular success story, Oprah Winfrey resonated across the whole world. This is a collection of proverbs that have impacted the lives of millions of people around the world:

- Live your life, and if you are open to the world, then you will learn how to live it perfectly.
- Every day brings you the opportunity to take a deep breath to make every moment in your life meaningful, and to enjoy every hour as if it were the last hour of your life.
- Life is full of joyful treasures, only if we give ourselves the opportunity to discover them.
- Rest assured, as there is a Lord for this universe, who will provide you with everything your heart wishes. Enjoy good, goodness, tenderness and love, and see what happens next.
- Do not live beyond your financial resources or in a way that only imposes burdens on you, so as not to live a lie you are not forced to believe.
- Gratitude changes any attitude, as it can move you from negative

energy to a positive one. It is the quickest and easiest way to make a difference in your life.

Funding

Ever since her youth, Oprah Winfrey has been averse to the idea of debt and to be indebted. Her father raised this feeling inside her from a very early age. He told her that debt generates a great imbalance in a person's life and a bit of laziness. When Oprah was away from her home and owed $1,800, she did not tell her father about that, because it was a failure for her. When Oprah could repay that debt, she promised herself not to buy more than she could afford.

"When I was little, I was a poor girl who was ethnically and gender-discriminated," says Oprah Winfrey. "Education is your way. If you have proven yourself and worked hard, then you will be able to reap substantial capital by having a good job or by excellence in your field."

In today's world, acquiring skills is very easy with the internet. Education is no longer the exclusive preserve of the rich like before. In the past, there was a widespread notion that the social capital of the rich was simply more effective than that of the poor.

Giving

Oprah was fortunate to be able to offer wonderful gifts, from bedding to university education. She has been able to donate homes, cars, and trips around the world, as well as the wonderful nanny services.

She talks about the real footprint that will be left to the people, who have seen her program over the years and whom she helped to return to school, lose weight, live healthily, stop beating their children or even skip a failed marriage. Oprah says merely that her heritage of all this is represented in the people who lived and tested her voice and words, that have already influenced them. The inheritance, as described by her, must represent the life of a person who was influenced, so that his life could be dedicated to serving as a beacon for others.

In 1997, Oprah founded her famous program, *Oprah Single Network*, which provides financial assistance to those in need. The program has achieved tangible results. Two hundred homes have been built to house the displaced. The program also included $ 30 million to create a university education grant for needy students, in addition to her moral and financial support to the victims of the *tsunami* through her network that aims at encouraging volunteerism. No one can forget the greatest humanitarian work of Oprah when she visited Africa, where she adopted 50,000 African children, as an attempt to contribute to

solving the chronic poverty problem of many children in Africa. She decided not to have children, and to focus on caring for children in need. In 2007, Oprah established a leading girls' academy in South Africa to provide talented girls from poor families with educational and leadership opportunities where they can then make a difference in the world and serve the community.

"We have all heard that you will feel happier when you give rather than take. Giving involves greater pleasure, and nothing makes me happier than a well-given gift, which is met with joy. I can honestly say that every gift I have ever given has brought me a degree of happiness that is equal to the happiness of its recipient. I give what I feel," Oprah says.

Lifestyle now

By 2018, Oprah Winfrey has a fortune, which is worth $ 2.7 billion, and has a diverse wealth of high-value assets, such as Montecito Palace in California, which is worth $ 100 million; a two-floor villa in Chicago, which is worth more than $ 5 million; and her property in the Hawaiian Islands, which is worth more than $ 32 million. She also owns a private jet. She has her *Harpo Group,* which includes houses for film screenings, as well as she has video companies that run Oprah programming which is viewed by people in more than 100 countries around the world. Oprah also owns many shares in *Oxygen Satellite Channel.*

As for her health, Oprah has many convictions represented in the diet. One of them is the importance of eating well. Eating a meal that brings you real joy will benefit you more in the long-term.

Oprah has learned to eat a maximum of one or two chocolate pieces and to force herself to eat and enjoy it. She says she does not have to eat the whole food just because it exists.

Howard Schultz
"The Emperor of Coffee"

9

Howard Philip Schultz, The Emperor of Coffee

Childhood and Family

Howard Schultz was born on July 19, 1953 to an impoverished family in Brooklyn, New York. His father was a US Army soldier, and his mother, a receptionist.

Howard had a brother named Michael and a sister, Rooney. Living in harsh conditions, the family could not pay for the cost of housing. As a result, they were forced to live in a housing under the Housing Authority in South-East Brooklyn.

At a very young age, Howard became a smuggler. This was due to the hardships he and his family underwent. However, because of his love for sports, he found solace in basketball, football, baseball – channeling his negative energies to positive ones.

In 1982 at 29 years old, Howard Schultz married Sherry Kirsch with whom he had two children.

While his wife worked on the interior design, both managed, to establish the Schultz Family Foundation in 1996, which raised the human spirit and gave the opportunity to all, regardless of skin color, religion or sex, Howard said, "We see the challenges our nation has

faced. However, if we work together to unleash our potential in our societies, then we can build a nation that fulfills its promise.

Education

In his high school days at Kanarsi, he had proven his athletic supe-
riority over his fellow students. This enabled him to obtain a special
scholarship for athletes from the University of North Michigan. As he
was the first to enroll in the university, he became a role model for his
family. He graduated with a bachelor's degree in telecommunications
in 1975 at 22 years old.

The beginning of work

When he reached the age of 12, Howard Schultz began his first work
experience. At the same time, he sold newspapers, and worked in a
small cafe near his home for a few years to provide for himself and his
family.

After successfully completing his university studies, Howard Schultz
worked as a salesperson of a coffee machine at *Hammarplast*, a Euro-
pean coffee maker in the United States.

With the promotion of *Schultz* in the company and his appointment as
a sales manager in the early 1980s, he noticed that he was selling more
coffee machines to a small company in Seattle, Washington, known at
that time as *Starbucks* (for coffee, tea, and spices) more than he was
selling to *Messi*. As a result, he decided to move to Seattle. Howard
Schultz later expressed this by saying, "Every month and every quarter,
these numbers were rising, even though *Starbucks* had only a few stores.
Therefore, I said to myself: I am going to Seattle."

One year after his first visit to the emerging Starbucks, Howard
Schultz became the sales and marketing director of roasted coffee beans.
"From my first step into Starbucks, I started to feel at home," he said.

Social Life

Howard Schultz was keen on spending most of his time at work every day. He did not consider his job as routine and pieces of work to do, but as an expression of his passion and a way to achieve his goals in life. The secret behind spending all his time at work was his enjoyment of the work.

Howard lived his life without any close friends, but his employees were always friends, as he often shared special moments that had nothing to do with work with them. He was keen on providing a workplace that promotes a family atmosphere.

Howard Schultz has been known as a positive personality full of optimism, ambition, kindness and love. These qualities build confidence, stability, growth and success, according to what Howard sees.

Staff

Jerry Baldwin, Gordon Bowker, and Zev Siegl founded Starbucks in Seattle in 1971. Howard Schultz had been the sales and marketing director for 11 years on its inception. The company then specialized in selling roasted coffee in bags for use domestically.

In 1987, Howard bought *Starbucks* and became its CEO. He developed *Starbucks* from selling roasted coffee beans to selling coffee in the shop.

Throughout his career at *Starbucks*, he has always given priority to his employees. He even called them partners, not employees. His love of his employees was translated into a system that works for them. For example, he provided them with full health care, and gave them the right to buy the company's shares.

Painful Past

On one cold winter day in 1960, Howard Schultz returned home from school, and found his father lying on the couch because of work injury.

He fell on a plate of ice, and broke his leg. He was merely sent home after the accident, dismissed from work without any compensation and health care coverage. He was a driver of a diapers delivery truck.

When his father died of cancer in 1988, he had left the family without any savings or pension. This taught Howard to provide his employees health insurance starting in 2009, which cost about $ 250 million a year. He managed to turn the pain he had suffered earlier by providing hope for others.

Challenges

In February 2008, Howard Schultz decided to close all the 7,100 branches of *Starbucks* in the United States with a sticker saying, "We need enough time to master black coffee, espresso." At that time, espresso had a specific mechanism for professional preparation. When espresso was prepared quickly, its taste would be light, but if it was prepared slowly, it would be too heavy. He realized that there was a group of *Starbucks* employees who were not sufficiently proficient in this preparation, which made him decide to close this large number of branches for half a day, to guide and train the staff using video recordings on the ideal way to prepare black coffee and espresso. A total of 7,100 videos were distributed among the Starbucks outlets nationwide.

This step caused the company to lose millions of dollars, but Howard was convinced that good work was better than making money. He said that the quality of the product and the customer's satisfaction were above everything. *Starbucks* was and still is, greater than just a company that offers coffee. "Without a great coffee, there is no reason for our existence." These were the words uttered by Howard Schultz after closing the outlets. He knew, and he was very certain, that this step was a risk. *Starbucks* had lost $6 million, as well as a number of customers who were offered incentives by opportunistic competitors during the half-day closure. However, with Howard's awareness of all these, he said, "I know that's the right thing I have to do."

Passion

Ever since he was young, Howard Schultz has been passionate, and this passion grew as he got older. He was so keen on making *Starbucks* a favorite place for everyone after home and work. This was his vision that he was working to achieve. He has already been able to achieve it.

Howard first discovered his passion during a business trip to Milan, Italy, where he saw that the coffee served was blended with love and positive energy, and a smile that helped customers enjoy their beverage. It has been clear to him that coffee is not just a daily routine drink by people, but it is more than that, as coffee brings people together in a quiet place; students drink coffee while studing their lessons; lovers drink coffee in a romantic atmosphere; and colleagues drink coffee and discuss the matters of work. This was what drives the passion of Howard. Through that, he wanted to create such atmospheres accompanied with the coffee provided by *Starbucks*.

> *Some of the most significant principles that Howard Schultz adhere to are:*
> *Discovering opportunities*

- Creating a strong team based on the company's love
- Maintaining the values and principles of the company
- Solving problems and not blaming anyone.

Dream and Goal

Howard's ambition has made Starbucks a famous international brand, and known to be a coffee company that inspires and nurtures the human spirit.

Ever since his first day at *Starbucks*, Howard Schultz wanted to establish that kind of company his father never had the opportunity to work for. As he puts it, a company that respects the dignity of work and the dignity of all men and women.

Howard's father's job termination without compensation and health care benefits despite work-related injury was a massive blow to the family. They had no money for his father's medical needs, no money for food and no money for other needs. Because his experience was deprivation of life's happiness, he vowed that in his time of success, no one around him would be exposed to such harsh realities and unfairness.

Turning Point

On a business trip to buy supplies and equipment for *Starbucks* in an international home appliance exhibition in Milan, Italy, he decided to tour Milan's coffee shops first. He watched baristas who work with high precision, artistry and skills, and how they made wonderful coffee. He wanted to bring this sophisticated and professional knowledge and skills in coffee preparation to *Starbucks*.

From this moment on, Howard decided that *Starbucks* sell coffee beverage, not just coffee beans. "I saw something fantastic not only in the romance with coffee, but in the sense of communication between people and coffee. A week in Italy, I became convinced of that idea, and felt so excited that I could not wait for my return to Seattle to talk about my plans for the company."

This was a turning point in his career. The Milan journey.

Persistence and continuity

Like other successful and leading companies around the world, *Starbucks* has suffered some failures, most notably in 2007. All shareholders, partners and even customers thought the company's demise was brewing because of Howard's decision to step down as the CEO of

Starbucks. He appointed a board member to be the new CEO.

However, all the staff and partners called for his return to his post because he was the best person to lead *Starbucks* to business security, innovation and reliability.

Howard did not hesitate to return to *Starbucks'* leadership. Upon his return, he hired consultants and began taking action to address the problem that the company was going through.

Among the most important measures taken were:

- Reducing costs and reducing the opening of new branches to improve the effectiveness of expenditures.
- Reaffirming the *Starbucks* values and principles at work.
- Some of the most significant quotes of his:
- What *Starbucks* offers is bigger than just a cup of coffee.
- Failure is not an option one can take.
- We're not in the business of filling bellies; we're in the business of filling souls.
- Making cuts on goods is not an appropriate strategy in the long-term.
- As a global company, it builds its brand upon an unlimited relationship with customers, a relationship of trust.

Success

Inspired by what he saw in Milan, Italy, he insisted on having Starbucks serve coffee beverage despite criticism and refusal of some stakeholders. However, success came after the mushrooming of *Starbucks* branches at 27,000 in 75 countries in 2017. It is still growing around the world employing 300,000.

"*Starbucks* is growing exponentially, opening two stores every day in different parts of the world," according to *Business Insider site*. This

success is not just personal, but also the partners' and the employees'. The employees have the option to buy the company's shares. They are covered with health insurance, a retirement plan and education tuition fees scheme.

Howard's father died before he could see what his son had done. If he were alive, he would be, according to Howard, proud of what he has done to the working class.

Funding

When Howard Schultz offered the founders of *Starbucks* the idea that the company would turn from selling roasted coffee beans to selling coffee beverages, the founders initially rejected the idea, the reason Howard was forced to resign from the company, and set up his own company, *The Journal.*

He wanted to achieve his dream through coffee at any cost. Howard encountered the challenge of collecting more than $1.6 million, from 242 people, including the 217 who rejected the idea. However, he did not think why some people rejected an idea he was certain about its success.

Sixteen months after the opening of the company, *The Journal,* he founders of *Starbucks* turned to him again and offered him to buy the company with its equipment and branches for $3.8 million. However, he bought *Starbucks* stores, for the same amount offered by the founders, and had it merged with his company, The Journal. As a result, Howard became the owner and CEO of *Starbucks*.

In 1992, Howard introduced *Starbucks* shares in the US stock market, earning him ample money.

Giving

Howard Schultz loves giving, and he, himself, is full of love for others. He has many stories detailing about the wisdom of giving. One such

story was in the African State of Rwanda, where Howard was on a business trip to visit coffee farms. He met a number of workers in the fields, and began asking them about their dreams. Everyone was disclosing his dream until a woman, named Mukamweza, talked about hers. Calmly, she told Howard that her dream was to earn money to buy a cow for milk for her family, and sell it to get more money. Howard replied that he would try to provide her with a cow. Indeed, after meeting with his partners in the *Starbucks Charitable Foundation*, they sent the cow to her house in Rwanda. The Starbucks Charitable Foundation was established in 1997 as part of their commitment to strengthening communities.

Lifestyle now

Howard has focused on providing healthy eating at *Starbucks*, believing that health is an essential part of anyone's happiness. *Starbucks* aims to make every customer happy, and not only fill his stomach.

In 2018, *Starbucks* has reached its 47th year of providing coffee to the world, 31 years of Howard's ownership of the company, and 37 million visitors per month in the US alone. Howard Schultz has achieved tremendous success by building an empire of coffee. He has a net worth of, according to *Forbes site*, $ 2.8 billion until mid-2018.

Jeff Bezos
"The Electronic Godfather"

10

Jeff Bezos, The Electronic Godfather

Childhood and Family

Jeffrey Preston, nicknamed Jeff Bezos, was born on January 12, 1964. His parents are Jacqueline Geez and Ted Jorgensen, who separated after a marriage that lasted only 17 months. His mother later married another man named Miguel Bezos, who legally adopted Jeff when he was four years old. He had a strong influence on Jeff's life, and made him carry his family name. Jeff lived with his mother and his stepfather in Houston.

Jeff Bezos says that one of the most significant education of his childhood was his summertime spent at his grandfather's farm, where managed his own affairs. He learned how to take responsibility for doing his own work without relying on others, and even learned how to value every second of his life.

On one beautiful day at the farm, Jeff was in the car with his grandmother. He heard a radio ad saying, "In every puff the smoker blows out of his cigarette, it takes a few minutes from his age." He immediately thought about his grandmother who is addicted to cigarettes. He counted the number of years she spent smoking so far. Then he counted the number of cigarettes she consumes each day, as well as the number of puffs per cigarette. He then quickly went to his

grandmother, and told her about the seven years she had lost in her life.

Jeff Bezos was not expected to be rebuked by his relatives, but praised for his intelligence, wit and arithmetic skills. This is because kindness is more important than being smart in dealing with others. This is one of the most important lessons he learned in his youth.

When Jeff Bezos was 29, he married a colleague. Then, he and his wife, McKenzie Bezos, together with their three children and one adopted daughter, moved to Seattle.

One of Jeff's main concerns in educating his children was to allow them to take risks, so that they were allowed to play with knives, believing that self-reliance teaches one resourcefulness, which he called "a major trait of business and everyday life." He repeatedly said, "Learning tricks at an early age helped him in business, especially when he founded *Amazon network*, where he faced frequent failures and had to take risks. Every time he faces those risks, he repeats, "When something delays me, I have to rely on myself and think outside the box."

Education

Jeff Bezos enrolled in the River Aux School in Houston, but did not spend much time there because his family moved to Miami, where he completed his high school at Miami Palmetto School. Then he enrolled at Princeton University in New Jersey, where he majored in computer studies, and graduated with a bachelor's degree in 1986. On every summer vacation, he would go to Norway to work as a computer programmer. He wanted to gain advanced experience and skills.

While Jeff Bezos was a college student, he used his spare time to work at a McDonald's restaurant. He recalls one of the situations he experienced during his shift: On one occasion, he accidentally dumped a large amount of ketchup in a hard-to-reach place in the kitchen, which prompted the administration to make him take the responsibility of cleaning by telling him, "Find a solution to reach that difficult place."

Jeff Bezos's teenage life was full of lessons. One of the most important lessons that inspired him to recommend for people of his age, who are about to enter the labor market, is they can learn responsibility while holding any office, if they take it seriously, in ways that exceed what one learns during his studies at school.

The Beginning of Work

Jeff Bezos had his first work experience at 16 years old. He worked in a chain of fast food restaurants. Then he worked for Vettel, a two-year-old startup. After that, he moved to his second stable job at *Banker Trust*, and on to *De Chau*, an investment management firm in Wall Street.

Jeff was obsessed with inventions and innovations, feeding his curiosity by doing so. He had a passion for determining things and knowing how things worked and he was always interested in taking a step ahead of others.

His obsession with technology has made him a person certain of making great achievements. He exploited the internet because of its great potential in networking. This led him to seek investment opportunities through the internet. The internet was a pioneering and innovated idea at that time. He was able to make that technological template, that has led readers to what they want by reading through cyberspace.

Although there was a large number of people involved in marketing and sales, many expected this idea would fail, but Jeff was determined to implement it. To establish the company, he would need a million US dollars. At his disposal was only a hundred thousand dollars he took from his parents. It was a struggle to convince investors to pour such a huge amount of money into his project.

Jeff took great pains in taking advantage of his relationships with some people when he was on Wall Street. He discussed the business potential of his project with about 60 investors to convince them to invest a sum of money in establishing *Amazon site.* However, the

comments of most investors were very negative. Precariously, he had already assembled a group of programmers to begin designing the website he dreamed of.

To persuade investors, Jeff used a research by John Quarterman, in which he said that the internet network increasingly grows and may grow to about 2330% annually. Jeff explained to prospective investors his business plans, and voila, the site was born!

Social Life

Jeff works very hard, but not necessarily addicted to work. He always starts his day by partaking healthy breakfast with his wife. He never schedules his meetings in the morning, so he can spend time with his family. When he returns home at night, he has dinner with his family and does the dishes. He considers this as one of the night tasks he must do before sleeping. He was also keen on getting a comfortable rest of eight hours each night until he wakes up without an alarm in the morning.

In an answer to a question about how he manages a balance between his family and business life, Jeff said, "I do leadership training courses for senior executives. This question is always addressed to me. In my view, I do not even like the term 'balance'. It is a misleading term. I love harmony in work and life because I know that if I work actively and happily in my work and feel that I am adding a great value to it and that I am part of the team, then this will, whatever increases your activity and energy, increase your activity and energy at home. You will be a better husband and father and vice versa. If I am happy at home, that will make me a better manager at work."

Jeff Bezos saw that the real thing is your energy. If your work absorbs your energy, or your work produces extra energy, then it is so at home. It is a circle that is not related to the balance of life and work, and is not concerned with the number of working hours, as Jeff has no problem in this aspect because the two sides increase his energy.

One of the habits that Jeff Bezos practised is meditation. He allows himself a few days a year to create a space for himself and for his ideas. These empty days, according to him, are the times when one tends more deeply toward his thoughts.

Staff

When Jeff Bezos interviews prospective employees, he classifies them into four categories:

- Must not be hired.
- Tends more to be not hired.
- Tends more to be hired.
- Must be hired.

When a person is hired, the recruitment criteria are raised each time a new employee is accepted, in order to increase the quality and develop the talent in the company.

Three (3) questions were identified by Jeff Bezos before he decides to hire any applicant:

Question	The objective of the question
Will I personally be impressed by this person?	That Jeff was impressed by those from whom he learned a lot
Will this person raise the level of effectiveness of the team?	Responsibility, partnership, integration and development
In what area will this person be excellent?	For more creativity and refinement of possibilities

Every time Jeff and his team appoint a new employee, he raises the

recruitment criteria the next time, so he can constantly develop the talent he has. An employee at *Amazon* must work for long hours, work hard, and work intelligently. He cannot be employed with only two of these three.

Jeff Bezos notes in his memoirs that his first official storeroom was part of a basement in a building that was windowless, where the *Amazon* logo began as a mere design of the river. By 2000, Turner Duckworth Agency had redesigned the logo, saying: The meaning behind the new slogan of Smile and Arrow is, "We are happy to deliver anything anywhere."

In a press release of *Amazon.com*, one of the retailers in the corporation said, "The smile is now under the letter A and ends under the letter Z," adding that *Amazon.com* offers everything from A to Z.

> *"The principles of our leadership are not just a wall of inspiration suspended at* Amazon,*" says Jeff Bezos, referring to* Amazon*'s employees. "They still have a wall where the principles of leadership have been suspended. These principles work just as hard as we do, as Amazon uses them every day, whether they're looking for ideas for new projects, deciding the best solution to the client problem, or interviewing candidates. This is just one of the things that makes* Amazon *a leader."*

- For an employee to become a leader in his work, he must have the passion for customer service and maintain confidence.
- For an employee to feel his ownership of the corporation, he has to believe in long-term goals and act on behalf of the entire corporation. They are those who cannot say, "This is not my

business."

- To improve the employee himself, he must be passionate about learning; must have curiosity about it; and must always seek to discover new possibilities.

Painful Past

The last time Jeff Bezos saw his father was when he was three years old. He, with his mother, moved to live with her parents after a marriage that lasted only 17 months. Jeff's father was an angry person, and agreed to divorce his mother without hesitation. In turn, he paid a small sum to support Jeff when he was a child. However, he failed to pay sometimes.

Jeff remembered his father briefly. As the years went by, he forgot him. In an interview with Jeff in 1999, he said of his father that he had never met him, indicating that his father left no impact on Jeff's current life. The father of Jeff Bezos did not know that his son was still alive and that he had achieved all that success.

Challenges

Many analysts predicted that Jeff Bezos would not be able compete with traditional stores when he launched *Amazon*, although he could overtake his rivals in a short time. In 1997, he officially announced his position to the public.

One of the main challenges Jeff learned during his work at McDonald's was to keep things going as quickly as possible, especially during stress, and this was the first learning experience for the world's richest man.

In his experience, Jeff Bezos points out that there are two kinds of criticism, and that the key is always looking at the mirror and making the decision, so the vision will show you whether your criticism is right, or not. If so, you have to change and not resist.

Passion

"Do something that you feel passionate about, and do not chase your temporary passion," Jeff Bezos often repeats such a saying when he talks about the importance of passion for talent and skill to anyone. Jeff has seen many people feel temporary passion and leave their jobs to do something on the internet, as what happened in 1849 in the Gold Rush incident, when there was a boom in gold exploration. Many people left their jobs and headed for the gold rush, but not all of them got the gold, although they all worked for it.

If we go back to that date, we will see that everyone has been affected by this passion; even the doctor has left his profession and went looking for gold. Oftentimes, those people do not succeed. Even if they did, they would not be satisfied with what they have done. One has to be clear with himself, as when he looks at his life in the 80s, he will reduce what he might regret doing or not doing. These principles help one in his decisions regarding work, but also at the level of family decisions. Jeff says in an interview that he has a 14-month old son. When he is 80 years old, he wants to see this young man grow up. Jeff does not want to regret not doing so.

Innovation and creativity were one of the most important qualities and skills of Jeff Bezos. He created the idea of *Amazon*, represented in selling books online. He began to expand his business in this electronic library. He started in 1998 with the introduction of videos and CDs after it was only limited to books. In 2002, he added the sale of clothing to his site portfolio. By 2007, *Amazon* had introduced the Kindle, which uses electronic ink to make reading easier.

In 2010, *Amazon* signed an agreement in which it obtained the digital rights of the masterpieces of the authors, which angered them because their views were not taken into account. However, with the increase of the readers and sales of books, that benefited them, made them change their minds. In 2013, Jeff launched a new experimental service, *Amazon Prime Air*, a service based on small and unmanned aircraft, which are capable of carrying small weights of up to five pounds and flying up to 10 miles to deliver orders to customers faster. After one year, in 2014, Jeff Bezos founded *Blue Origin* for aviation, which developed some techniques to provide space flights for customers. It remained secret until a plot was purchased, upon which he built a testing and launching

facility he owns.

Dream and Goal

Jeff Bezos, the founder, and CEO of *Blue Origin*, has great ambitions for the human race. His vision is for millions of people who live and work in outer space. Jeff said at a press conference that *Blue Origin* will launch a new missile factory in Cape Canaveral, Florida and that the space tourism activity coming from *Blue Origin* is the starting point for Jeff's big vision. The vision was that reusable rockets would be able to significantly reduce the cost of launching, making space travel affordable to people interested in booking."

Two months after that press conference, Jeff Bezos said that *Blue Origin* had successfully tested its concept by launching a rocket and landing it after launching a capsule on the edge of space. This is a great and unprecedented achievement the company has achieved in aeronautics and space science.

Turning Point

No one denies the genius of Amazon's founder, Jeff Bezos, who has made spectacular successes with this store, which is based in its infancy on selling e-books. No one denied his wits when he decided years ago to break into the tablet industry. They are modern devices that operate with the touch and fingerprint system. Consequently, he was able to achieve successes that have forced competitors to focus on the segment of high-quality and cheap tablets.

However, Amazon, which lost $ 400 million because of breaking into the sector where competition does not have mercy on no one. We are talking here about the smartphone sector as the company tried to launch *Amazon Fire Phone*, but this product failed to attract sales stronger than expected, because of the vast production costs that almost threatened the financial stability of this global corporation.

Jeff has been strongly smacked when he saw this failure, which came after a long process of success.

In a statement to the event, Jeff Bezos noted that the failure has led to a radical shift in his acceptance of failure despite successes, and said, "You have to embrace failure." Jeff learned from this experience that what really matters is that you have to continue to experience new things. Companies that do not adopt failure reach a miserable situation.

Persistence and Continuity

"No, I did not expect Amazon to achieve this scale of success. This is normal and expected for each area of work. The beginnings are small and sometimes weak. Then, step by step, the size of the company increases. Companies also pass successes and failures. However, we must stand and ask what needs to be done to overcome these failures.,"

Jeff Bezos said in response to one of the questions asked in an interview about whether *Amazon* was expected to achieve that rapid success.

Success

Jeff Bezos has acquired a great deal of success, and investors are going to his office to convince him to invest their money in his company. After his success, Jeff believes that it is dangerous to get to the stage of professionalism, and to act on it, as one may fall into the trap of science and knowledge. Jeff advises everyone who seeks promotion in his work, to have his seeking as the curiosity of a child and as the knowledge of an expert, but with the mind of a novice who is eager to know more.

Jeff Bezos always repeats the following statement: The choices are who identify you, not talent. Jeff implies that when one wants to make an important decision in his life, he can choose a relaxed and comfortable life, or a life full of adventures and unpredictability.

Jeff Bezos put forth a philosophy called 'the first day.' This philosophy came in the early days of the founding of *Amazon*. What it means is the company should always be in the status of the first day in terms of enthusiasm, effort and strength. Jeff attributes much of the concept of the first day of this philosophy to the success of *Amazon*.

Funding

It was Jeff Bezos who founded *Amazon*, and assumed the position of its chief executive, who initially supported the company himself for $10,000. During the first 16 months of the foundation, he funded his project with an additional $ 84,000 through interest-free loans.

There were only Jeff and his table in the garage. His parents invested in *Amazon* in 1995 for $ 100,000, although he had told them that their chance of losing would reach 70% in that investment.

Giving

The first gift given by Jeff Bezos after his remarkable success at *Amazon* was his $10 million donation to the Fred Hutchinson Cancer Research Center to launch a program for expanding the use of certain types of immunotherapy for breast, ovarian and prostate cancer. He gave another $ 20 million for this work in 2014. By 2017, Jeff gave $ 35 million to the same center.

In 2011, Jeff presented a $ 15 million grant to Princeton University to help establish the *Bezos Center for Neural Circuit Dynamics*, focusing on a relatively new area of research called connectomics. The center includes neural measurement and connection for data to better understand the brain. These data may be critical in understanding and treating a variety of neurological diseases.

At the level of support for the education sector, *Bezos Foundation* has donated millions of scholarships, both large and small. Each year, it funds the Bezos Scholars Program at Aspen Institute.

Migrants had a share of Jeff Bezos's support, as he had donated $ 33 million to the Dreamers Scholarship Fund for immigrants to America in childhood, with more than 1,700 immigrants.

Lifestyle now

Jeff Bezos made a fortune of $ 132.2 billion in May 2018. As for the health aspect of his life, he admitted that his eating habits were not very good. He ate a full packet of biscuits at breakfast every morning. His wife finally managed to stop him in one day and asked him to read the ingredients. Jeff, who said he was thin as a railroad at that time, said, "I never read any food label in my life." His wife, McKenzie, helped him put an end to the unhealthy breakfast routine. Since then his physical transformation has begun.

11

Algorithms: Statistics and Graphs

C ongratulations to you, dear reader, for reading these rich stories of the emperors of wealth. Our trip was wonderful along with nine different characters, whose stories were classified on a set of points, all centered around fifteen points regarding the emergence and stages of life of these characters, with all the variables and challenges that prompted them to refine their potential existed in the depths of each of them, until they have been embracing major global achievements that had great impacts over a wide range of humanity from various experiences.

In this chapter, entitled "Algorithms", all nine stories you see yourself will turn into tools that have the magic effect of changing your life. The language of words is understood by the right mind, as the letters are stacked together, and the words are composed of meanings that tell you consistent stories of giant tycoons. You will now turn to algorithms that contain numbers, drawings and tables that are understood by the left mind, which more systematically and more concisely responds to them. This chapter will address your left brain more than the right one, as you have finished reading all the stories that have addressed your right mind until you have known the results these characters have reached, after a trip of rich life. This new chapter will work to create a balance in the information you have, where it will make you re-read the stories, but briefly represented in diagrams,

tables and graphic illustrations with numbers.

It is very important to be aware of this chapter well, and focus on the diagrams presented in it. We will work here to facilitate all the diagrams that will pass in this chapter, which will allow you to answer all the questions that have been brought to your mind about the findings of such characters in this book. Those characters will be placed under the microscope in one space, so you can see them more clearly and more accurately, which will help you to understand the latest essence of this book.

Graphs

After reviewing the data and highlighting the observations and the fifteen points, and after they had been compiled and sorted, this chapter collected the most important details mentioned in the success of the characters dealt with in this book, and then it compared such details about the characters with one another, in a way that illustrates the foundations on which the wealth of these characters was built, which lets you analyze and discover the path to wealth and the conditions on which it is built.

The first point: childhood and family

1. This diagram shows the stability of the social situation in the childhood of each of the mentioned characters and shows how social stability affects success.

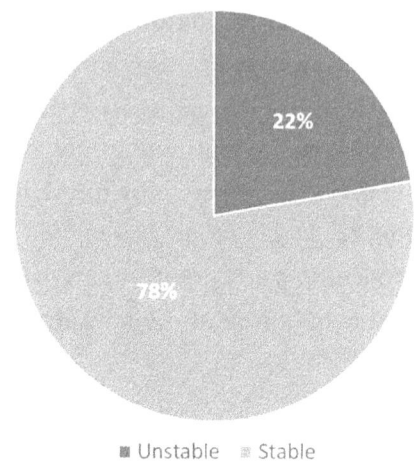

Was the social situation stable in childhood or not?

2. This diagram illustrates the diversity of the material status of the households of the characters.

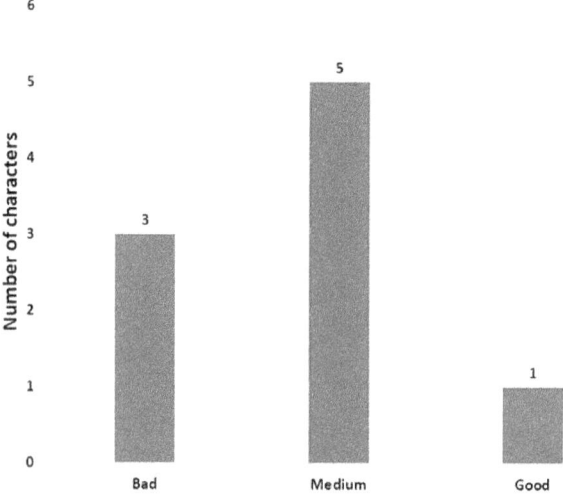

What is the economic status of the households ?

3. This diagram compares the age of marriage among the mentioned characters.

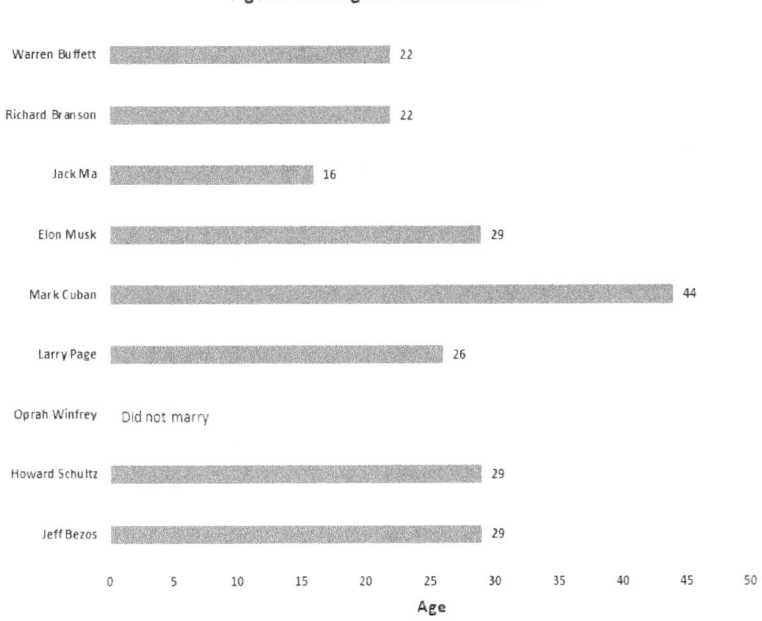

Age of marriage of the characters?

4. This diagram shows the influence of the parents on the characters in determining their field of work.

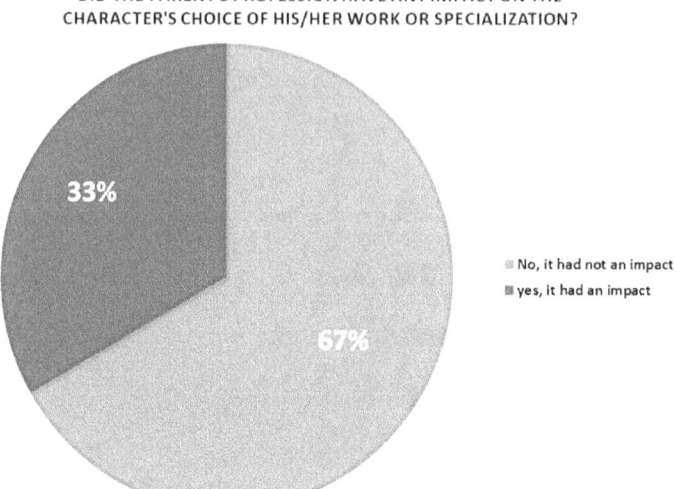

The second point: Education

1. This diagram shows the percentage of the characters who have completed their college education.

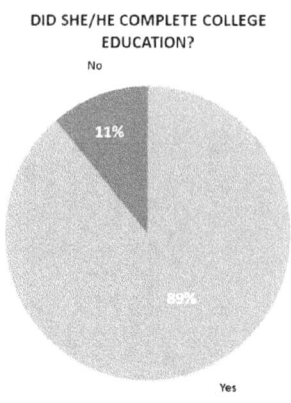

2. This diagram shows the educational level of the characters.

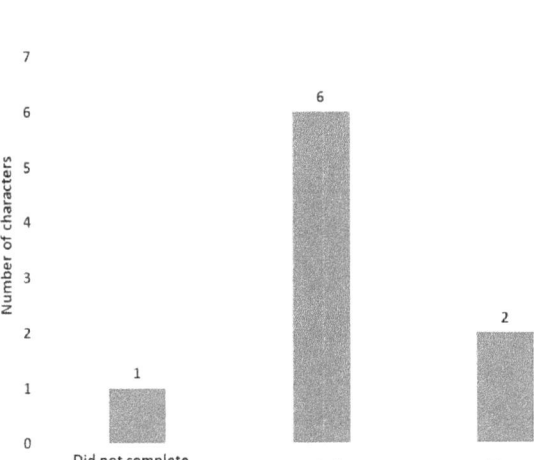

Character's educational level

3. This table shows the college specializations of the characters.

College Specialization	
Character's Name	Specialization
Warren Buffett	Business Administration
Richard Branson	Did not finish school
Jack Ma	English language
Elon Musk	Physics and Economics
Mark Cuban	Business Administration
Larry Page	Computer sciences
Oprah Winfrey	Theatrical Arts
Howard Schultz	Commucations
Jeff Bezos	Computer sciences

The third point: Beginning of work

1. This diagram shows the ages of the characters when practicing their first job as employees.

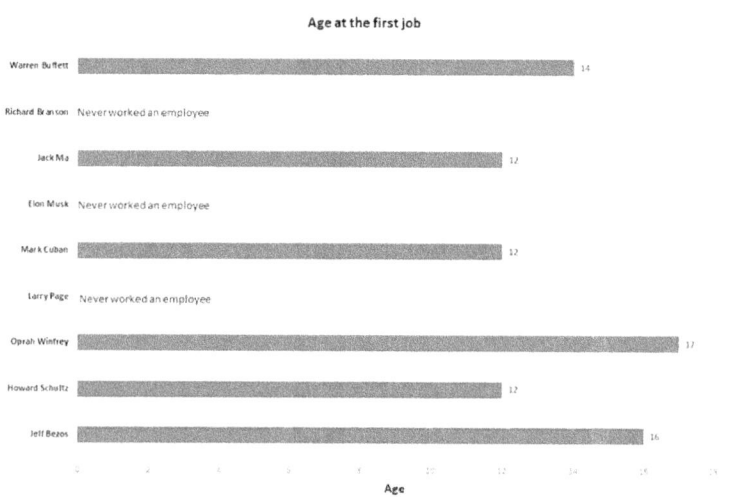

2. The following table shows the type of job that each character worked in:

The first job each character worked in	
Character Name	Type of employment
Warren Buffett	Selling papers
Richard Branson	Never worked as an employee
Jack Ma	Tour guide
Elon Musk	Never worked as an employee
Mark Cuban	The seller of garbage bags
Larry Page	Never worked as an employee
Oprah Winfrey	Broadcaster on a local radio station
Howard Schultz	Selling papers
Jeff Bezos	A worker in a fast food restaurant

This diagram shows the age of the characters when the company established its first commercial project.

The age of the character at the beginning of his/her first project

Age

3. This table shows the type of first business each character worked in:

The first project founded by each character	
Character Name	Type of project
Warren Buffett	Selling soft drinks and chewing gum
Richard Branson	Magazine
Jack Ma	E-market
Elon Musk	Games on the computer
Mark Cuban	Selling baseball cards
Larry Page	Search engine
Oprah Winfrey	TV studio
Howard Schultz	Coffee shop
Jeff Bezos	E-market

The fourth point: Social life

1. This diagram shows the number of characters and their relationships with friends.

130

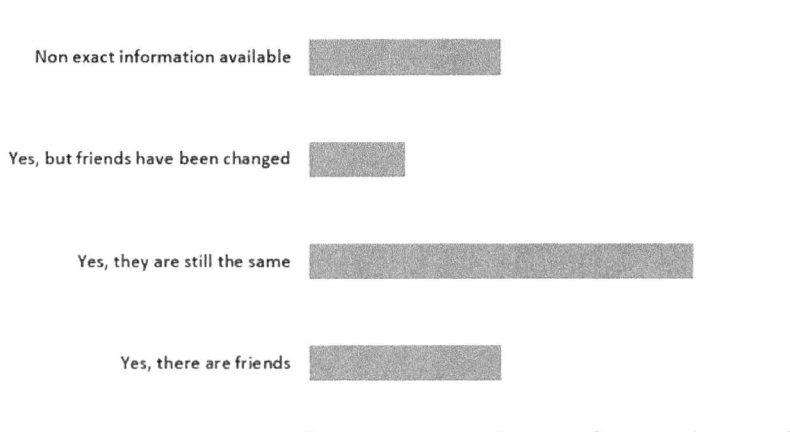

2. This diagram shows the percentage of the characters whose friends have been involved with them in their businesses.

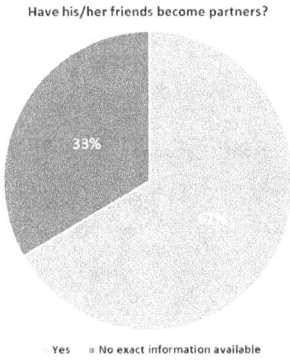

The fifih point: Staff

1. This diagram shows how the characters deal with their employees.

How was the treatment with staff?

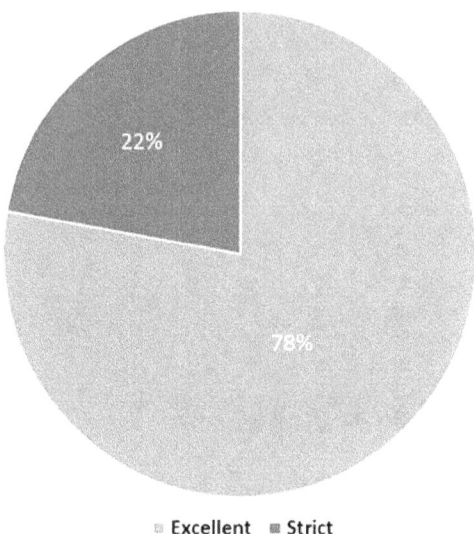

⊟ Excellent   ▪ Strict

2. This table shows the characteristics that each character cultivates in the work environment.

What does the character try to cultivate in his/her staff?	
Character Name	**The characteristics**
Warren Buffett	No exact information available
Richard Branson	Having fun at work
Jack Ma	Smiling
Elon Musk	Learning, risk, and love of work
Mark Cuban	Having fun at work
Larry Page	Creativity
Oprah Winfrey	Optimism and hope
Howard Schultz	Their love and loyalty to the company
Jeff Bezos	Creativity and work under pressure

3. This table illustrates the characters' selection of their employees.

What do the characters look for in their staff?	
Character Name	**The Characteristics**
Warren Buffett	looking for integrity, intelligence, and high energy
Richard Branson	Looking for who can perform the tasks better
Jack Ma	Looking for who can perform the tasks better
Elon Musk	looking for integrity, intelligence, and high energy
Mark Cuban	Looking for passion and commitment
Larry Page	looking for personality, knowledge, and experience
Oprah Winfrey	no exact information available
Howard Schultz	Looking for the employee's personal compatibility with the values, principles, and vision of the company
Jeff Bezos	looking for educational qualifications

The Sixth point: Painful past

1. This table illustrates the diversity of the pain that has affected the lives of each character.

What was the pain that affected the character's life and career?	
Pain	Character Name
Warren Buffett	censure by his mother
Richard Branson	no exact information available
Jack Ma	facing rejection constantly
Elon Musk	Financial and personal losses
Mark Cuban	financial status
Larry Page	no exact information available
Oprah Winfrey	family status
Howard Schultz	family status
Jeff Bezos	family status

2. The following diagram shows the age at which the characters experienced the pain that has affected their lives.

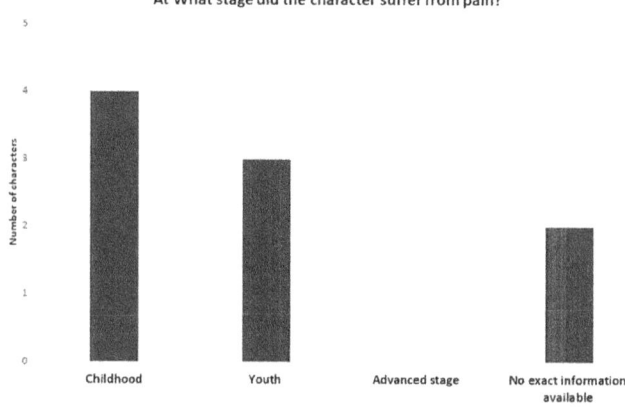

At What stage did the character suffer from pain?

The seventh point: Challenges

1. This drawing shows the adherence of characters to their projects when encountering failure and their ability to refuse to abandon them.

Has s/he abandoned the project in which s/he failed?

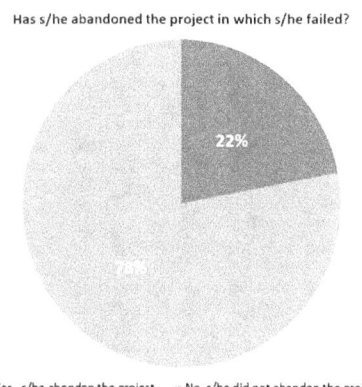

■ Yes , s/he abondon the project   ■ No, s/he did not abandon the project

2. This diagram shows the types of challenges experienced by the characters mentioned.

Type of challenges s/he encountered?

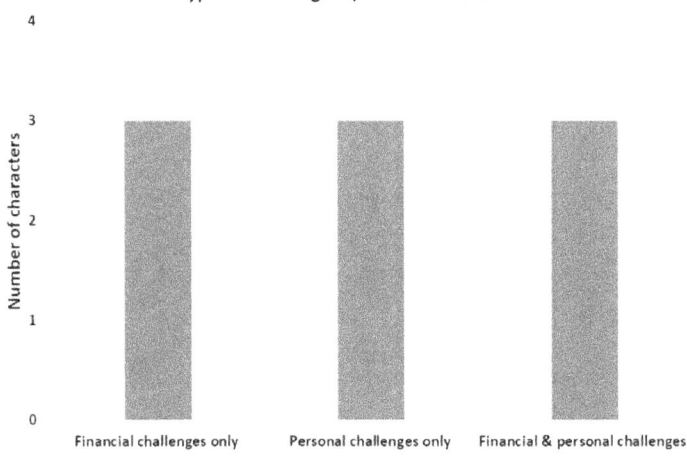

The Eighth point: Passion

1. This diagram shows the percentage of the characters who invested their talent in their projects.

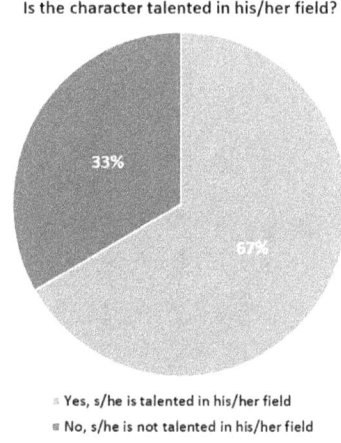

Is the character talented in his/her field?

33%

67%

⬜ Yes, s/he is talented in his/her field
⬛ No, s/he is not talented in his/her field

2. This diagram shows the percentage of characters that turned their passion into a project.

Has s/he turned his/her passion into a project?

100%

⬛ Yes ⬜ No

3. This diagram shows the percentage of the impact of skills on the success of characters.

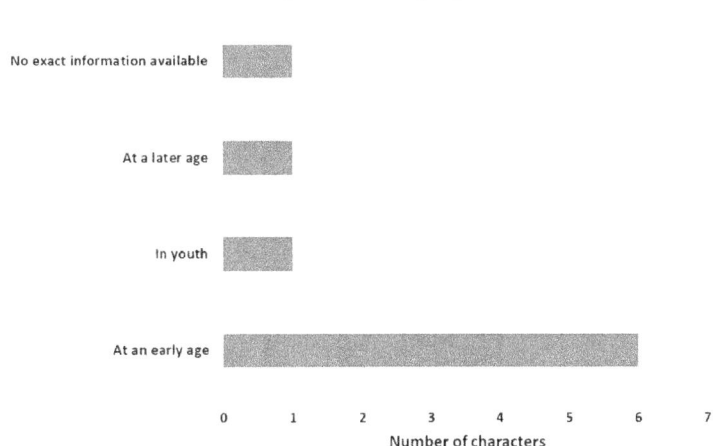

Has s/he turned his/her passion into a project?

100%

Yes   No

4. This diagram shows the age in which the characters knew their passion.

When did s/he discover her/his passion?

No exact information available

At a later age

In youth

At an early age

0   1   2   3   4   5   6   7

Number of characters

The ninth point: Dream and goal

1. This diagram shows the percentage of the compatibility of characters' projects with their dreams and goals.

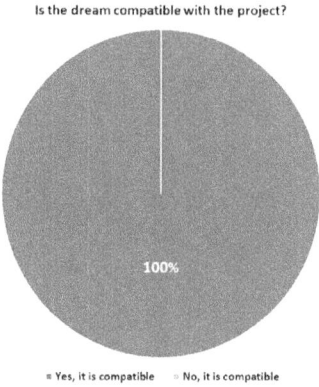

Is the dream compatible with the project?

100%

▪ Yes, it is compatible   ▫ No, it is compatible

2. This diagram shows the characters' commitment to writing down their dreams and goals and announcing them.

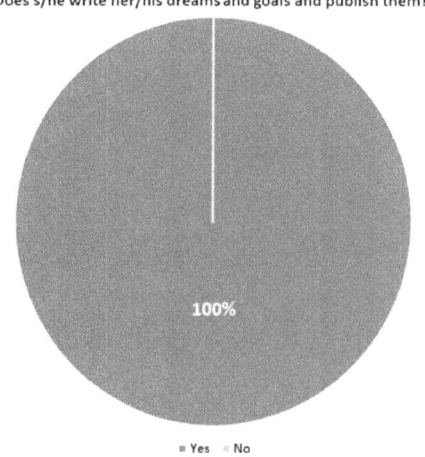

Does s/he write her/his dreams and goals and publish them?

100%

▪ Yes   ▫ No

3. This diagram shows the characters' commitment to achieving their dreams and goals.

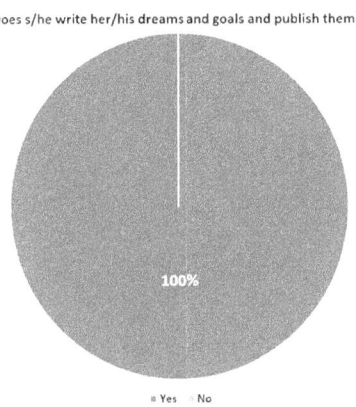

Does s/he write her/his dreams and goals and publish them?

100%

Yes No

The tenth point: Turning point

1. This diagram shows the type of the incident that led to the character's success.

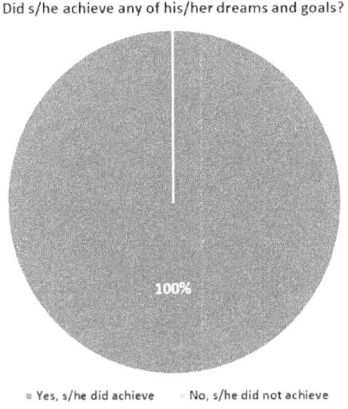

Did s/he achieve any of his/her dreams and goals?

100%

Yes, s/he did achieve   No, s/he did not achieve

2. This diagram shows the source of the turning point of the characters.

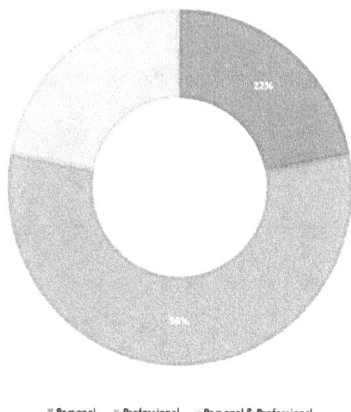

CLASSIFICATION OF THE SOURCE OF TURNING POINT

22%

56%

■ Personal   ■ Professional   Personal & Professional

3. This diagram shows the time range of the impact of the turning point on the characters' success.

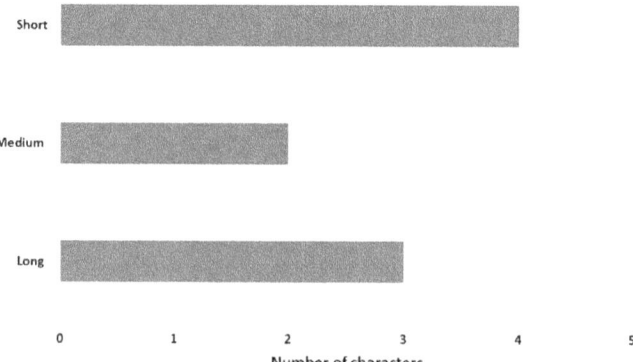

The duration of the impact of the turning point on the character's success.

Number of characters

4. This table shows the time period between the turning point and the characters' success.

What was the duration of the effect from the turning point?	
Character Name	Duration
Warren Buffett	6 years
Richard Branson	3 years
Jack Ma	4 years
Elon Musk	2 years
Mark Cuban	7 years
Larry Page	4 years
Oprah Winfrey	2 years
Howard Schultz	7 years
Jeff Bezos	No exact information available

The eleventh and twelfth points: Persistence, continuity, and success:

THE AGE OF CHARACTERS IN THE STAGE OF BUILDING WEALTH

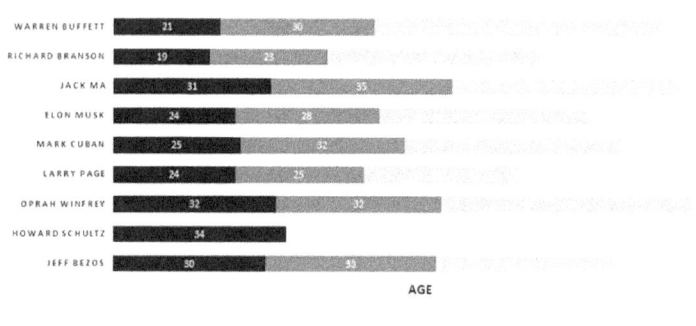

■ Characters age when founding the project (year) ■ Characters age when achieving first million (year)   Characters age when achieving first billion (year)

This diagram shows the age of the characters in the stages of building wealth.

The Thirteenth Point: Funding

1. This diagram shows the sources that the characters used to fund their projects.

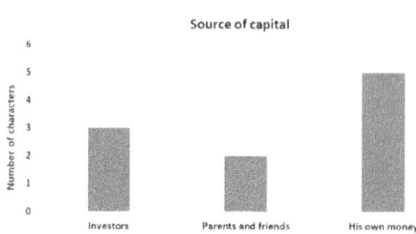

The fourteenth point: Giving

1. This diagram shows the importance of giving to the characters.

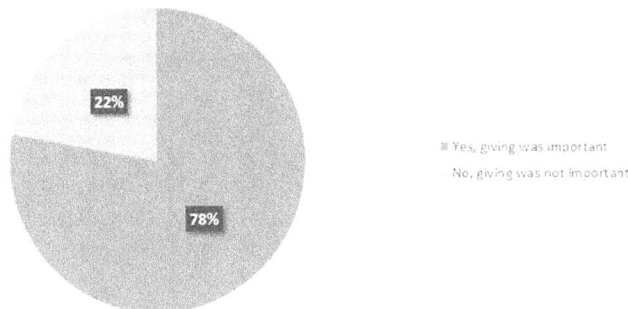

Was giving important for character in her/his beginnings?

22%

78%

▓ Yes, giving was important

No, giving was not important

2. This table shows the parties to which each character directs their donations.

Which aspect in which the character is interested, concerning bestowing and giving?	
Character Name	Side
Warren Buffett	social , educational and health
Richard Branson	environmental, social
Jack Ma	environmental
Elon Musk	scientific, health
Mark Cuban	Social
Larry Page	health, educational, social, environmental and scientific
Oprah Winfrey	social , educational and health
Howard Schultz	social , educational and health
Jeff Bezos	social , educational and health

The Fifteenth Point: Lifestyle Now

1. This diagram shows the wealth size of each of the characters mentioned.

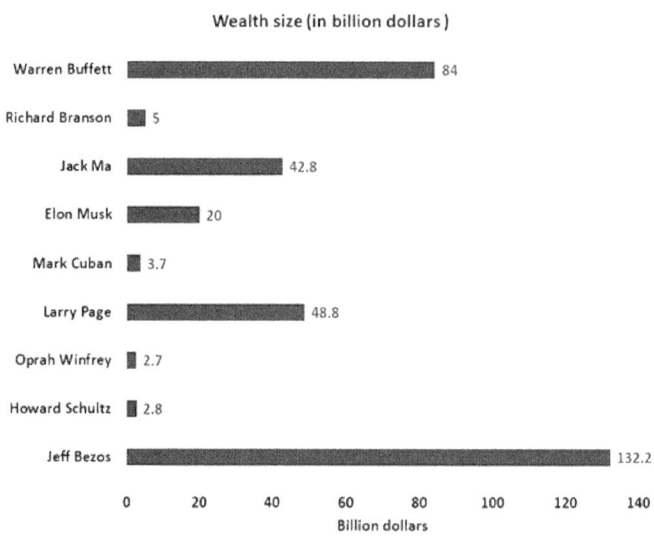

12

Microscope X15: Analysis and conclusion

O ne of the most important things implied in the stories of the emperors, who built themselves on their own, are those events and circumstances that correspond to what any entrepreneur comes across in his early days, as well as the solutions that led to the success of those wealthy persons, which can be reproduced in order to achieve results similar to or better than their success. It is noted in the previous chapters that with the diversity of the selected group of the wealthy, we have found points of similarities and differences through which we can conclude the formula of wealth and follow the roadmap to success. These points were counted in fifteen key elements, and then we put them under the microscope of this book. The following are the analyses and conclusions of this research.

Childhood and Family:

A. The environment:

If we look at the upbringing of each of the selected characters, we will notice there is a difference in the surrounding environment, as there is a good environment and a bad one. Every character lived in a different family situation. Family stability was not a factor of success, and the disorder was not an obstacle to the realization of their dreams.

B. education:

The educational aspect differed from one character to another, but the only important similarity leading to the success of the wealthy is the implantation of self-reliance and responsibility. Each of the characters had a situation in which he developed a sense of responsibility and self-reliance.

C. Material status:

The material status of the family of each character has played an important role in cultivating the basic principles of wealth in their lives. It was a fundamental reason for each of them to know the importance of money, making their style of dealing with money more balanced, which has contributed to the expansion of perceptions of the characters to access the means to get money at an early time of their lives.

D. Love of selling and responsibility:

These wealthy personalities found pleasure in selling and passion in the early stages of their lives, which showed their real awareness of the importance of money, which helped them build the skill of selling. The market is divided as a seller and a buyer. If you choose the side of the seller, you will be the one who controls the material aspect of your life. As Mark Cuban says, "It is not important what you see in the cup if it is full or empty, as this is what the buyer does, but it is important to be the one who controls the content of the cup and who spills in it."

Education:

Level of education:

The educational factor has been an influential factor in the lives of most wealthy persons, as they have emphasized the importance of educational attainment. However, the uneven level of education among the characters makes it a clear sign that scientific achievement and the fetish about education are not enough to be a factor of success.

A. Scientific level:

We see that all nine selected characters have obtained a university degree, except Richard Branson, which proves that the impact of

education on success lies not in a university degree or specialization, but in the person's desire to learn and develop his skills at the school of life.

B. The effect of university education:

The real impact of university education on the success of characters was to learn skills and expand into the areas in which every character was so influential, such as Larry Page, Warren Buffett, Jeff Bezos, and Marc Cuban. We see a clear link between their specializations and their own projects. Warren Buffett, who started investing and trading since he was young, attributed his success to Benjamin Graham, who met him and learned from him the art of trading and picking the winning stocks. Larry Page and Richard Branson took advantage of the learning period to form relationships, which later built relationships between them as that of Larry Page and Sergey Bryan, through which the search engine, *Google,* was launched.

C. Continuation of education:

There is a complete consensus by all the characters mentioned in the book on the continuation of education even after the completion of the stages of education, and on its importance in constant self-development, which led to subsequent successes and achieving goals.

The Beginning of Work:

A. The purpose of work:

All the characters stressed that their successful work was not based solely on making money. Despite their awareness of the importance of money in the continuation and success of projects, the objectives of their projects carry a completely different dimension. Some projects were created to achieve lofty goals, and others were created to solve individual problems. Unifying the objective was a key factor for them, as we learn from the stories of those characters that the first signs of success are when all employees and partners work on the same goal upon which the project was set up.

B. The first practical experience:

One of the most important factors of success is trial and experience. The wealth of rich people at an early age is the result of their practical experience in dealing with money and trying to get it at a young age. Risk and how much experience contribute significantly to the expertise needed to make the right decisions. Warren Buffett is the first to handle money. He started at the age of seven. The majority of the characters worked at a young age of 16, but that was not an obstacle to Larry Page, who started his actual career when he was 24 years old.

C. Do they work in a field they love?

All the characters have pointed to the importance of doing what you love and loving what you do, and this is one of the matters agreed upon, in addition to the urgent need to spend a lot of time building their assets, which makes doing what you love and loving what you do something important and essential, because you will spend a long time at work and you may go through many difficulties.

Social life:

A. How they were dealing with their friends:

A similar trait of these characters is that they love to celebrate, spend time with their friends, maintain their friendships for a long time, seek new friendships, and expand relationships, which had an impact on their ability to earn material and moral support to realize their dreams and develop themselves. Because there is no perfect human, using your relationships can fill in what you lack, multiply the effort and reduce the time required in productivity. Increasing your acquaintances also makes it easy for you to reach those who are in dire need of your services or supporters who can help you build your business.

B. daily routine:

There is a strong relationship between being rich and getting up early, as most of the rich wake up early because of the high productivity at that time, as we have reviewed in their stories. We saw that Jack Ma and Richard Branson both wake up at 5 am. Elon Musk also wakes up at 7 am. The behaviors that are agreed by these characters are their

interest in work, as their first job is usually to peruse their business, such as replying to their e-mails. Exercising sports is also one of the priorities of their morning tasks.

Staff:

A. Enjoying work:

All the characters emphasized that enjoying work was an important aspect, and pointed out that the working environment should be a safe, comfortable and harmonious environment for all, in order to be a successful environment.

B. Dealing with staff:

There is a complete agreement on the importance of exchanging love with employees to all the selected characters, which supports the creation of a comfortable and loving work environment, which increases stability and increases the efficiency of work, but even goes beyond the practical environment to reach its impact on social life, as known about Howard Schultz and Richard Branson, who love celebrating with their employees and sharing special events, which contributes to building a practical environment as if it is one family. It was also said that supporting staff and helping them to develop their talents, just as what Jeff Bezos and Jack Ma did, is essential to the development of the employees themselves and their key to start their own journey of richness.

C. How they select employees:

One of the most important qualities of the nine characters is to find the right person to be in the right place in terms of the skills required for any person applying for any job with these characters. These characters are also keen to raise the standards related to employment to boost the performance of their corporations.

D. Dealing with customers:

Winning customers' love and loyalty has also been an important factor in the success of these characters. We see that clearly in their

principles and goals. We also recognize that protecting customers is the first principle of all their projects, so they keep their customers and aim to satisfy them, even at the expense of their success or critical times of work.

E. Their responsibilities towards employees and customers:

All the characters agreed on the importance of supporting employees and creating a working environment for them. Richard Branson and Howard Schultz explained the employer's relationship with employees distinctively, as the stability of the employee's life is mainly based on the continuity and success of the project, as well as the factor of mutual love lets the employer fight for the sake of success and continuity, which explains the connection between success and continuity and love of employees.

Painful Past:

A. Suffering:

The lives of these successful characters have not been without painful experiences. This indicates that their life is swinging, just as what happens with anyone. Rather, in some cases, these painful experiences exceed the ordinary stages of any human being, which makes overcoming these obstacles a source of inspiration for others.

B. Solutions:

With every pain in the lives of the rich, we find that the trait of search and the creation of solutions is one trait, which is agreed by all the characters, which indicates that the rich lack the concept of surrender, and this makes them in a continuous pursuit of success. Despite the importance of focusing on solutions by 80%, these characters do not miss facing problems, even if it is by 20%, without complaining in order to find a radical solution to the problem. Without considering the problem and facing it, the solution is not radical, but remains a partial solution.

Challenges:

A. Belief in the goal:
The nine characters were similar in their faith in the goal, making it easier for them to focus on successes and meet challenges more strongly.

B. Overcome all challenges:
It is interesting that, with the impressive successes of each individual, and with the constant search for solutions and the unwillingness to surrender, they have not been able to overcome all challenges and experiences, which is a clear sign that they are not miraculous.

C. Dealing with failure:
Despite the trait that the wealthy do not surrender, the acceptance of failure is also a common trait among them. They are similar in the way they deal with their challenges, which is represented in accepting failure, admitting mistakes, taking responsibility, and correcting the course.

Passion:

A. Passion's relatedness to success:
The passion factor is also a common factor in all characters. First, they started with ideas they were passionate about, and this justified their ability to spend a lot of time working and trying to gain the skills needed to achieve their project goals.

B. Talents and their relationship to wealth:

Talent may not be the basis for success, but it plays a significant role in facilitating success as we see Oprah Winfrey, Larry Page, and Warren Buffett. The basis for success, as can be deduced from the nine characters, is the skills acquired in pursuit of the goal, which reinforces the idea of continuous learning and continuous development of all successful characters.

Dream and Goal:

A. The objective of the project and work:

With the full belief that money is one of the most important elements of success for each project, most of the projects mentioned above have other goals that focus on providing a service or solving a problem. These goals have a strong relationship with personal experiences. The need of a person to get some service or confront a problem was a source of ideas and projects. The success of their projects relied heavily on their experiences and expertise.

B. Focusing on the goal and its relationship to success:

Focusing on the goal has a strong connection to success, while the loss of focus is one of the first elements of failure in any project. This is what we see clearly in the previous narration, where we see Howard Schultz when he came back to lead *Starbucks*. The first thing he did was correcting the course and returning to goals which *Starbucks* adopted, and we see the focus on the target as a reason for Elon Musk's success to overcome the pain of failure in his first three attempts to launch his space rocket. We see also Richard Branson that when he lost his goal, he was about to give up his empire. When his dreams and goals returned, he returned to work and developed, so that his works could leave a major imprint on human life.

C. Money as a goal:

At the same time, and in a state of equilibrium, money was not the first goal of any of the wealthy projects, but it was one of the most important goals. The wealthy celebrate gaining money and celebrate their other goals, which is a clear sign of their full awareness of the importance of money as a pillar of the project.

D. Writing down dreams and goals:

The nine characters differed in their way of writing down their dreams and goals, but agreed to do so. Every one of them wrote his dreams periodically, ranging from annual to monthly. Rather, that reached a higher degree as in the status of Elon Musk, who divides his day

precisely to cover his commitments in pursuit of his dreams.

Turning Point:

A. Admitting mistakes and correcting the course:

Admitting mistakes and taking responsibility is the first step to encounter the challenges. The idea of correcting the course has been repeated in all the tips of the wealthy because it reduces the impact of risk and indicates the activation of the continuity of learning, experience, and clarity of purpose. This indicates the feature of modesty and lack of arrogance and acceptance of criticism for those who wanted to move forward for the sake of success.

B. Belief in the idea:

The faith in the idea of each of the nine emperors was not the only motive to start the project but was a factor of continuity and acceptance of risk. In most cases, where the rich have to abandon or sell his project, it does not mean abandoning the idea or the goal by which they began their projects.

C. The relationship of the turning point to wealth:

The challenges and incidents of each of the nine emperors have made them accept failure, correct the course and seek solutions, and make these incidents a turning point in their lives. This has directly led to the rapid promotion of these characters into wealth, as we see that the period between the incident and the success did not exceed three years like what was mentioned in the story of Richard Branson.

Persistence and Continuity:

A. The feature of stubbornness, initiative, and risk:

The rich have focused on several important features they mentioned in their advice, which makes it easier for anyone to succeed. The most important of which are their stubbornness, initiative, and risk. Risk and initiative help overcome the unknown and seize new opportunities,

which made them entrepreneurs and more advanced than others. The belief in the idea and stubbornness is the protective shield of various and repeated frustrations, because the belief of the nine characters and their aspiration to success is greater than the frustrations experienced by entrepreneurs, and we see that clearly in their repeated rejection and objection.

Success:

A. The concept and measurement of success:

There is a complete consensus on the concept of success of the wealthy, as they emphasized that their successes are linked to achieving their goals, not the size of their wealth. Measuring successes was through the effort to achieve the goal, not through the number of hours spent in the work as described by each in his own style.

Funding and Capital:

A. Source of capital:

The sources of capital are divided into two main parts; private money on the one hand, and investors and loans on the other hand, in a seemingly contradictory fashion, but its real content is perfectly compatible. Most people when they wanted to start their own business from scratch, they sought to attract investors, starting from friends and family to borrowing from banks, foremost among them Warren Buffett, who raised $ 105,000 from his family, while he did not pay more than $ 100 from his own pocket. The other side, such as Oprah and Marc Cuban, opposed the idea of borrowing and built their projects from their own funds.

B. The relationship of the investor to the entrepreneur:

Mark Cuban justified his refusal to borrow from investors by carefully explaining the investor's relationship to the entrepreneur as weak relationship, just as what Richard Branson, Larry Page, and Elon Musk

experienced, as they suffered from a lack of the decisive decision in their projects and in their exclusion, but this did not prevent either party from achieving their successes.

Giving:

A. The source of giving:

The rich did not deal with giving and charity to others as a bank that provides money to society, but they considered that as a responsibility and a project like any of their own projects. Those projects were based on ideas and experiences passed through the lives of each of these emperors, and it is noted that the idea of spreading happiness and saving the world are not ideas underestimated by the wealthy, as the majority of them are interested in giving, but this is conditional to them, as it should be organized and in the form of a project and in an ongoing institutional framework. Each of these characters is interested in the details of this giving, such as the size of the public interest and the continuity of the project, as this is clear in the development of education and clean energy.

It does not require success to be successful, and it is not necessary for a human to be generous for the sake of success, as Richard Branson and Warren Buffett have proved. The first began the journey of giving before the dawn of success, and the other did not start his journey until his wife inspired him by her charitable deeds, but we see clearly that the rich deal with their charitable projects exactly as they deal with their own private profitable projects. The approach leading to the success of the profitable project is the same approach leading to the success of the charitable project.

Lifestyle Now:

A. Healthcare:

The idea of health care among the characters ranged from doing sports to a healthy diet, but they did not lose interest in regular health examinations like Warren Buffett, which saved him from cancer by early detection, which made his recovery possible, which led him to be still healthy to this day.

B. The relationship of employment age to the age of wealth:

The employment age of the nine characters is not related to the speed of wealth, but the apparent connection is related to the young age of employment and the maturity of the investment mentality, as a result of the multitude of experiences passed by the character. It is also evidenced by search the link of the fast achievement of wealth to the speed of the spread of the project.

C. The source of the first million dollars:

The number one million is one of the most important barriers in the world of wealth. Crossing the barrier of million is the first threshold of wealth, but in view of the nine characters, they were divided into two categories; the first category has achieved great success in their work after an effort, as happened with Jeff Bezos, Richard Branson, and Warren Buffett, raising their own profits to over $ 1 million. The other one made a strenuous effort to attract investors to whom they sold their successful project in a satisfying amount, and they have surpassed the barrier of $ 1 million, such as Mark Cuban and Elon Musk.

D. The source of the first billion dollars:

The $ 1 billion barrier is a new barrier that the world's wealthy have been able to overcome. For the nine characters, the only way to reach and overcome this barrier is by accumulating money-generating assets.

Our Next Station:

Through the chapter "Microscope 15x", we learned about the information that led to success and richness under the different circumstances of all nine characters, as well as the difficulties and challenges that these characters have been able to achieve.

In the next chapter entitled, "The Harvest of Emperors", we will

discuss the conclusions of our previous reading and deduction, regarding the characters in this book, through a review of essential tips and pivotal keys, that enable you to make your way steadily towards achieving your true wealth, based on the basics, principles and values of the rich characters, about whom we have sailed in various aspects of their lives until your way to become like them is possible, in case that you follow the recommendations and advice you will read in the next chapter.

13

The Harvest of Tycoons: Recommendations and Tips

1-Childhood and family:

We often see people blame their past and blame their childhood or their families as if they are the main reasons for our current lives, especially with regard to our material status.

However, after we have done a deep search into the childhood and families of these nine characters who have achieved spectacular global successes, we came across those who had wonderful and exciting childhood and their families raised them in a good way, as well as their childhood and families were normal and similar to most families' lives. We have dealt with those who were suffering in their life under extreme poverty looking for a living. However different the past of these characters, there is what is common, as all them have succeeded and achieved huge financial wealth..

Our advice to you is that your success and wealth today is totally unrelated to what you have experienced in your childhood and what happened to your family in the past. Rather, your success is in your hands. You are the one who can achieve success and wealth for himself, not your family nor what you experienced in your childhood. Do not blame your past, but look at it only to learn

the most important lessons and experiences, in order to manage to work for building your wealth. Even the children of the wealthy encounter difficulties as young as the poor. The types of difficulties may vary, but at the end they are difficulties. Therefore, Know that everything happened in your past life, whether positive or negative, is only to prepare you for what will come and for the future.

2-Education:

We have dealt with different ways of how successful students got knowledge. Some of them got it from practice, experience, reading or watching the successful ones. Some of them learned from a situation, they did not expect to learn from, the most important lessons in their lives.

We see that the means are different, but what it is common is that all these characters have their constant desire to learn, develop and grow in order to achieve the goals they aspire to.

As for college education, this type of education is one of many tools a person can used to be rich, but it is not the only way to be rich. If you are going to join a university, or you still study at university, then continue, because it may help you develop the skills needed to succeed, but make sure that it is not the only way to be rich.

*   **Our advice to you** *is that success and wealth only come when you are ready to receive them, but preparing for them should be through learning and practice in order to apply what you learn. Always strive to develop yourself, to develop your life to the best, and to be keen to specialize in the field you love, as this love helps you to professionally perform to manage to build your own project. If you want to start your own project, you can certainly start it, even if you have not completed your university studies. Make sure that the best way to have good learning is to continue to search, to read books, or to watch videos; and to continue to get*

into experiences and other matters that concern your project and the mechanism of its operation and practice. The best step is to plan and start because once you start, you will learn more and develop through practice. If you do not practice nor apply what you learned, then this is consumption of your time and not an investment. Therefore, be careful not to consume your time in that which you do not have the result you aspire to. Keep learning and practice and do not stop. When you are ready, wealth will automatically come to you.

3-Beginning of work:

You have passed, through reading the stories of the nine emperors dealt with in the book, by nine different beginnings. It may not be the beginning that has achieved this magnitude of success at the present time, as some had a beginning that was the biggest failure to him, but even in cases of failure, those characters have learned from that failure valuable lessons. The beginning of each character is different from the other. We cannot guide you in what you are going to start now, and your start will often be different from those characters, **but our advice is:**

to start where you find your passion and where you can serve people or solve a problem they experience. In exchange for the service you offer, you can get paid for it. When this service is linked to your passion, then you will be on the right path to wealth. The size of your service to people equals the size of your wealth and success.

4- Social life:

"Tell me who your friend is, then I tell you who you are."

160

If you are a friend of seven people, who are bankrupt, then you will be

their eighth in bankruptcy, because the time you spend with them is spent with their ideas, concepts, interests, concerns and other things that indirectly affect you. Choose to make friends with those who have experience more than you and those who seek to build their wealth, because you will learn from them and their experience, which will affect your quest for wealth in a positive way. If you cannot find such people around you, then you can accompany rich people through what they have written by themselves or what others have written about them and through their video clips and other things that will add to your journey towards wealth. Make your accompaniment of these materials within your daily work.

How can you improve your diary?

Simply compare the diaries of the successful and yours. You will see that they spend their day at work, learning, developing, meditating, reading, and recharging their energy and other things. Ask yourself the following question: Are most of my diary spent to reach the goal I aspire to? Or most of my diary is spent on what I do not have any benefit or result? I do not mean to give up the things you enjoy, because enjoyment and times of joy increase energy, but you must invest most of your time to reach your goal by success in your wealth project. Time is the only element that cannot be compensated; if it goes, it will not return. Therefore, invest it in the best way, because what you do daily, even if it is simple, it becomes very useful and valuable over time.

Our advice to you is to copy the successful diaries to achieve your goal and to be close to those who will contribute to your development and help you develop, succeed and be rich. Therefore, the decision is up to you. All human beings have 24 hours a day. There are those who have reached billions, and others who are complaining most of the day about the high temperatures of the atmosphere and traffic congestion in the road. Therefore, the decision is up to you.

5-Staff:

Collaboration is the title that we can call the relationship of successful characters with their staff. Without the high performance of staff, you will not get a great result. If your relationship with them is characterized by affection, encouragement, respect, cooperation and other positive things, employees will love their workplace, and they will be keen on it, which will reflect on their performance, and thus, you will get a better result. This is what we have observed in the relationships of successful characters with their employees. They choose whom they need, even if they are better than they are. They choose who will be a good addition to the company, so that they can live up to the level at which they are at a better and higher level.

> ***Our advice to you*** *is if you are still working in your job and do not have your own company, start treating your partners as you would like to be treated, because one day you will have your own company and then you will have experience in dealing with partners and employees. If you are a company owner today, we advise you to treat your employees as you would like people to treat you, and to look at them as your partners with whom if you meet you can become a reliable and consistent team, that can achieve great achievements. Choose that who will be a good addition to the company and will develop it.*

6- Painful past:

All the characters we talked about suffering in one of the stations of their lives, and now they remember those pains and see the lesson and wisdom they have learned in those stations and painful situations.

If you are suffering today or have experienced a painful past, then know that you are not the only one who experiences that. There are those who have suffered and complained, and there are those who have suffered and learned but turned that suffering and learning into a great success that resonated across the world. What do you want to be?

Our advice to you *is to look at those pains that you have come across, in order to learn lessons and judge them. The lesson may be to learn patience, endurance or money management; or to learn how to control your feelings, work under pressure, or accept the loss and learn from your mistakes. There are a lot of possibilities. You have to consider these pains as making us stronger and better people, just as they have made those characters what they are today.*

7- Challenges:

Challenges are a natural part of the journey of wealth. Without challenges, you will not be able to develop. As we passed by the characters, we saw them all, without exception, having various challenges. If you want to be rich, you have to know that there is no fixed roadmap, that guides you to success, for the success of your project. The road is not decorated with flowers and trees to harvest its fruits, but you have to plow and then plant your seed, and then you have to be patient to reap its fruits. That seed needs water and sunlight. However, it may not bear fruit if the land is unfit for cultivation.

Our advice to you *is to consider the challenges as part of your journey to success and wealth. With each challenge, you will learn lessons. The bigger the challenges are, the more lessons we learn, and the lessons will ultimately make you harvest your seeds. Enjoy them because challenges can teach you more valuable lessons than success.*

8-Passion:

Love what you do and do what you love. All the characters in this book were passionate about what they were doing. Without passion, they would not have borne the challenges encountering them. Without their passion for their ideas, they would not have believed in their ability to succeed. Through their working with passion, they could be able to

build wealth.

It is true that passion alone is not enough to build wealth, but without working with passion on your project and idea, you will certainly not succeed and be rich.

Talent is the thing in which you are naturally masterful. Therefore, make use of your talent if it is appropriate to support you on your journey in order to reach your goal.

If you do not know where your passion is, then look for it and continue experimenting and perusal, because you will know it through experience, and then embark on the path from which you will gain wealth because of the support of the passion that was generated within you.

9-Dream and goal:

A dream is a thing you aspire to reach and achieve. The goal is the dream itself, in addition to putting it within a time plan to determine when you want to achieve that dream; do you want to achieve it after a year? Five years? Or you are used to laziness, and thus you will continue to delay it and say, 'If you do not achieve it within ten years, I will achieve it in the next 50 years, and if I do not achieve it, then I will try after my death in the other life.' You will not give up procrastination and postponement and thus your dream will remain just a dream cherished by you, without being achieved on the ground. These are the characters you passed by, and if your current status is better than one of them when you started, surely you can achieve your dream, as no difference between you and them, rather your current situation may be better than them today! You have no excuse to stop your dream. No one else will achieve your dream, because you are the only one who is responsible for your dream and the only one who can achieve it, no matter how old you are. If you are in the 20s, do not say that there is plenty of time, but go on and enjoy the rest of your life with your dreams. If you are in the early 60s or even older, do not say that it is too late because there are those who started at this age and achieved their dreams. There is something that combines the dreams of those characters, which is that

their dreams were related to providing services to others. Among those emperors are those who have passed sixty, seventy and eighty years old and are still working on achieving their dream and satisfying their passion.

Our advice to you is to put your dream into a specific time plan, so that you can know when you want to achieve it. Start by putting it in a short or medium-term plan; what will you achieve after a year from now? Then make a long-term plan; what will you achieve after five years from now? Then put the plan that leads you to this goal. This plan must always be scalable or changeable in order to discover the way that leads you to this goal, whatever happens. Rememberthat yourdreamislinkedto givingsomething to others, because the wealth of these emperors came when they helped others, and thus they got the income they deserved, as this helped them build their wealth. What is the plan by which you would help others in order to build wealth within one to five years from today?

10. Turning point:

Turning points may be positive or negative. They may come from your family or community or even from yourself, and that incident, idea or attitude is what plants something in your current time. These are lessons you have obtained and may be the most important in your life as the main pivot which turns you from one status to another. You may not have passed a turning point that you can remember now, or it may be your turning point today as you read this book or later. The turning point or the moment of transformation may come from where you do not expect, such as when you have a unique project opportunity.

Our advice to you is that it is very important to acquire that lesson that you will always remember in your life and make it a valuable benefit in your personal and practical life. Always be aware of

what is going on around you to interpret the events and deduce the wisdom that lies within them. Do not let life, with its days and weeks, go on, while you are preoccupied with the pain of the past or worried about the unseen of the future.

11. Persistence and continuity:

You will not reach any goal you seek one day without persistence and continuity, as they are two key elements to reach your goal. Success and wealth have a price; because there is no shortcut to wealth. Therefore, you have to persist and insist on what you want, learn in your way to it and learn lessons from the mistakes you may make, but you should not allow yourself to run out of patience and then surrender in the middle of the way. If you give up, then the percentage of your attainment of wealth is zero%, that is, you will not achieve wealth, you will not reach your goal, and you will remain in your place. On the other hand, if you had the determination and continued to seek to be rich, then your achievement of wealth will range from 1 to 100%. Whatever the number is, it is worthy of persistence and continuity, because if you achieve your goal, then you will completely change your life, and you will contribute to the change of the life of those around you to the best.

Our advice to you is that you should insist on reaching your goal and continue to do so, no matter what obstacles you are going through. Do not care about those who frustrate you, take you back with their words, or take you entirely away from your goal. Just go ahead with your determination and persistence to reach your goal with your full focus, because all those who have achieved success were persistent and insisting on achieving their goals.

12-Success:

Let me tell you the truth. Success is not easy especially at the beginning, where you will go under difficult conditions and obstacles, difficulties and mistakes and many unusual things. If success were

easy, you would see most people succeed and achieve their dreams. Success is not easy, and that's what sets it apart! Today you want to achieve success and achieve your dreams and goals and get your wishes. Of course, you have to pay for it. During your journey to success, as we read together in the stories of the characters, you knew that they had learned and developed and were better than they were because of their extraordinary journey to success.

The nine characters and other successful ones have all gone through difficulties and obstacles, but they have continued, and have not surrendered. That is why today they are successful.

Do you know why these characters continued and did not give up like most people? They did that because success is a goal for which it is impossible to live without achieving it. Success has not to be a wish you hope to get, just as most people who surrendered or failed to realize their dream, or even they did not try to pursue it, because their dreams and goals were a desire they wanted; if it is met, they will be happy with that and if it is not met, there is nothing wrong with what they have achieved previously and then they continue their life as it is. Successful people need success, and success for them is an urgent need they cannot live without.

Our advice to you is that success and achieving your dream, and your goal should be a need and not a desire. What distinguishes you as a human being from other creatures is a success. Success is your duty and not an option for you. You have created a human to seek, develop and build up, not to live a normal life you are not satisfied with. You were designed to succeed.

13-Funding and capital:

We often hear from people this sentence, "I cannot start my project because I do not have enough money to start." In fact, from our reading about the nine characters, some projects do not require capital. If they do, it is not necessarily to be yours, as you can start your project and get

money from the customers you serve. Then that money can be invested in your project. Therefore, you will not need capital.

There is another option: If capital is really a necessity to start, you can present this idea to the right investor who would like to invest their money in a great idea that could bring them more money. All you have to do is to be well-prepared to present that distinctive idea.

However, keep in mind that investors will not give you money, because your idea is unique, but they will first assess the person they will invest their money with. They will see you; are you a leader and can you lead this project to success? Do you have the ability to implement the investor ambition and achieve the income he expects from you? Or will he replace and exclude you from the project, considering that better for him? This is one of the most important elements for any investor, and then they will look at other elements such as the idea, the feasibility study, the project goal, etc. Therefore, you have two options to start your project without having money.

Our advice to you is to seek to build your business without relying on investors' money. Try to start your project, based on profits *from customers, and then reinvest your profits in the same project to grow, develop and make more profits. If your idea requires capital, you have the second option of offering it to the right investors. They may agree, and they may disagree, but do not give up and always think about solutions.*

If you have enough money, but you do not have the right idea to launch it, there are many people who have great ideas looking for those whom they will fund in order to be rich and successful, and there may be those looking for you to fund them to create the largest global company in the future, just as Amazon and Google.

14. Giving

What is common among the nine characters is that they all are not only thinking about their own personal interests but also thinking

and planning how to create an addition to others. Their investment and charitable projects began as that; how they can contribute to development to the best, as all of them have a high balance from massive donations, or through their own charities, or by their material support to areas that provide assistance to others. These acts make them feel happy. It is true that giving helps others and serves them. At the same time, it gives the provider psychological support, comfort and happiness. Giving is not associated with money alone. Counseling and volunteer work are all charitable activities practiced by the nine characters in the field of giving.

__Our advice to you__ is to be a most giver and start to train yourself on giving and to lead your project of giving, just as your other investment projects, in order to possess that rich spirit. This can be done by giving others your time, knowledge and expertise that help them; providing money to those who need it; as well as other things that you can give to others.

Keep in mind that the wealthy who have built their own

wealth have the spirit of giving and they are not thinking of only themselves, but they are eager to give and benefit others, to provide them with what they could never get. If you can manage your giving correctly, then you will manage your investment correctly. Do not fool yourself by saying, "When I become rich, I will give," as most people who say that sentence is bankrupt. Now you have identified the cause of their bankruptcy. Giving is not money you put in the pockets of others. Preferably, it is an investment that makes your world a better place.

15-Lifestyle Now:

There is a rich man who spends the rest of his life lying in bed, and thus he lives the life he does not wish for. Another one is in full health, but he is in financial distress, and thus he lives the life he does not wish for. A third one cares about his health, earns money, and therefore he

lives the life he so desires.

Our advice to you, on your way to wealth, is: do not be like the first one who sacrificed his health because of his preoccupation with work for the sake of money, nor the second one, who cared about his health at the expense of wealth, so that the quality of his life could be affected, but be as the third one, who earned health and wealth, and lived with whom he loves, with his full health and wealth. You may think that if you put all your energy and health without caring for them, you will get richer in a faster way, under the pretext that your interest in health will waste your time, but what is the point of being rich if you are lying on the bed? If you are in good health, wellness, and energy, this will give you more focus and energy to work to be rich faster, just as the nine emperors did. They all care about their health and work to increase their wealth.

– The Last Message –

Like the rest of mankind, the issue of wealth still fascinates me strongly and drives my passion. If wealth is a dream, it can be turned into wishes by reading and talking about it and imagining it in daydreams. Wishes can also be translated into planned goals with a clear timetable, view, and vision. Then, all of these plans, goals and wishes supported by passion can be turned into a tangible reality.

There's something you must know. When we searched and read the biographies of the rich characters, who are inspirational to us, and when we saw a very large number of videos and interviews of them, and after reading the biographies of the characters chosen carefully and then the team summarized and revised them in this book— I am still overwhelmed with some mystery on how we become rich like them. Their biographies were written as clear and accurate stories, drawn in graphs, their information was counted, and they were analyzed until we extracted recommendations and advice from them.

After a lot of meditation, we advise you here to know the following:

No one can develop something without knowing that which he wants to develop. One cannot develop anything about which he has no information. There are a lot of precious books in the science of wealth and money, which have added a lot to us and to others, we know, in their lives, such as George Clason's The Richest Man in Babylon, Napoleon Hill's Think and Grow Rich, T. Harv Eker's Secrets of the Millionaire Mind: Mastering the Inner Game of Wealth, Robert T. Kiyosaki's Rich Dad Poor Dad, The Business School, and Cashflow Quadrant, and Richard Templar's The Rules of Wealth, as well as a wide range of books of high value in the leadership and management of corporations and companies, and books of success and self-development.

To get rich, you have to pay the price in advance, and the first thing you learn is to turn yourself from a person, who thinks and wishes, to another one, who executes. Money does not come to inactivity, but to movement. The more you move, read, learn and begin your first steps of execution, the more opportunities will flow. Your income and life level is equal to your being as a human, who has the knowledge, savvy and ability to work, execute, endure and be patient, develop your skills, change your habits, and monitor your behavior. Compare yourself with yourself every day and add a little new value to yourself.

In conclusion, I will ask you very important questions: When will you become rich? When will you seek that rich day and night? How long will you be willing to spend your life without the money that will bring stability to you and to whom you love? Would you make this book like the other books you read, closing it and starting another one, without taking any step towards any opportunity that may bring you wealth or give you the chance to apply what you have learned from books and your experience? Do you want to spend your life deceiving yourself that you are still not ready to start at least the first step? Before you put this book down, I invite you to take the decision to start, not to return to the whirlpool of life, and to seek to perpetuate your name among the tycoons. Just before you start anything, **say 3, 2, 1 and start.**

Finished, praise be to God!

Research Team…. Thank you!

Members of the research team of "Enrich Your Life" after the last meeting of the team on 31 May 2018.

- Standing from right to left: Ahmed Saleh, Mohammed Nabhani, Osama Al-Sayed, Bara' Khan, and Ibrahim Saleh.
- Seated from right to left: Munira Al-Sahaf, Rashed Al-Nabhani, Omar Al-Rayes, Omar Al-Kooheji, Manal Al-Qattan.

www.ingramcontent.com/pod-product-compliance
Lightning Source LLC
Chambersburg PA
CBHW071303220526
45468CB00001B/252